Asian Arguments

Asian Arguments is a series of short books about Asia today. Aimed at the growing number of students and general readers who want to know more about the region, these books will highlight community involvement from the ground up in issues of the day usually discussed by authors in terms of top-down government policy. The aim is to better understand how ordinary Asian citizens are confronting problems such as the environment, democracy and their societies' development, either with or without government support. The books are scholarly but engaged, substantive as well as topical and written by authors with direct experience of their subject matter.

About the Author

TOM MILLER is managing editor of the *China Economic Quarterly*, published by research company GK Dragonomics, and a former Beijing correspondent of the *South China Morning Post*. Tom has a degree in English from Oxford and an MA in Chinese Studies from the School of Oriental and African Studies in London. After teaching for a year at Shanghai University, he studied Chinese at Beijing Language and Culture University and at China's Central Academy of Drama. Resident in China for more than a decade, Tom lives in Beijing with his wife and two children. This is his first book.

CHINA'S URBAN BILLION

*The story behind the biggest migration
in human history*

―――――――――――

TOM MILLER

Zed Books

LONDON | NEW YORK

for Jesse Burke, 1974–2012

China's Urban Billion: The Story behind the Biggest Migration in Human History was first published in 2012 by Zed Books Ltd, 7 Cynthia Street, London N1 9JF, UK and Room 400, 175 Fifth Avenue, New York, NY 10010, USA

www.zedbooks.co.uk

Designed and typeset in Monotype Bulmer
by illuminati, Grosmont
Index by John Barker
Cover designed by www.alice-marwick.co.uk
Printed and bound by CPI Group (UK) Ltd,
Croydon CR0 4YY

FSC
www.fsc.org
MIX
Paper from
responsible sources
FSC° C013604

Distributed in the USA exclusively by Palgrave Macmillan, a division of St Martin's Press, LLC, 175 Fifth Avenue, New York, NY 10010, USA

A catalogue record for this book is available from the British Library
Library of Congress Cataloging in Publication Data available

ISBN 978 1 78032 142 4 hb
ISBN 978 1 78032 141 7 pb

Contents

Acknowledgements

This book can trace its origins to a conversation with Dakis Hagen on a road somewhere between Cape Town and Port Elizabeth in June 2010, during the first week of the football World Cup in South Africa. Dakis told me it was about time I got off my backside and wrote a book. I put this idea to a friend and China author. 'You should write one,' he said. 'But be warned: writing books ends in divorce.'

A few months later, I was in Paul French's office in Shanghai blagging contacts for an article I was researching about Chinese retail. He mentioned he was looking for writers to contribute to a new series, to be called Asian Arguments, for Zed Books in London. 'I'll write one,' I said, without thinking. 'All right,' Paul said. 'Send me a proposal.' Three months later, I had a deal.

I do not intend to write an exhaustive list thanking everyone who had a hand, either directly or indirectly, in shaping *China's Urban Billion*. But it is appropriate to thank the people who were there in the beginning: Dakis Hagen and Paul French. In particular, I owe a debt of gratitude to Paul, who pushed my book from the start and was a supportive presence throughout the publishing process. And I must also thank my commissioning editors at Zed, Jakob Horstmann and Tamsine O'Riordan, for taking a punt on a first-time author and getting the book out so quickly.

The following people helped make the book happen: Chris Buckley, David Cowhig, Peter Foster, Peter Goff, Fergus Naughton and Konrad Shek. Valuable contributions were made by my colleagues at GK Dragonomics, especially Will Freeman, Alanis Qin, Rosealea Yao and Janet Zhang. I also benefited enormously from the discussions on Rick Baum's CPol listserv, which pointed me towards sources I otherwise would not have found. I am especially grateful to Andrew Batson, Kam Wing Chan, Matt Forney, Jes Nielsen and David Wilder, who read and commented on the draft manuscript. And special thanks are due to the dozens of people all over China who were so generous with their time – especially Chen Fangyan, Yu Changjiang and all the Li family in Dazhangshan.

On a personal as well as professional note, I owe a special debt of gratitude to Arthur Kroeber, my boss at GK Dragonomics. Back in 2004, Arthur took the unfathomable decision to hire an innumerate literature graduate with no prior interest in economics or business to report on, comically enough, economics and business. Without him, this book could never have been written. On a purely personal note, manly hugs go to all the Footy Boys (you know who you are) and Sausage Club (ditto) for keeping me sane in Beijing with beer and vulgarity.

And, finally, the biggest thanks of all go to Flora – simply for being there. The book is finished and I am still married. What more could a man ask?

Tom Miller
Beijing, May 2012

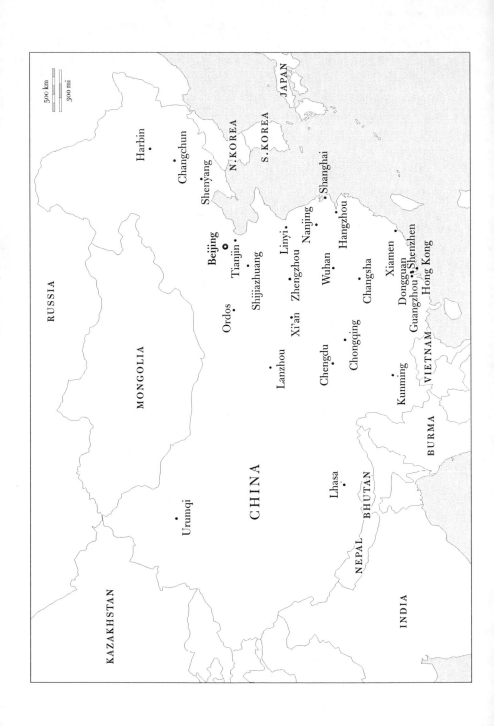

INTRODUCTION

The Biggest Migration in Human History

The journey from farm to city is the story of China's transformation from a poor and backward country to a global economic superpower. By 2030, when China's urban population is projected to swell to 1 billion, its cities will be home to one in every eight people on earth. How China's urban billion live will shape the future of the world.

Nowhere is China's urban miracle more obvious than in Chongqing, the largest city on the upper reaches of the Yangtze River. Once a rusting laggard, marooned far from the dynamic cities of the eastern seaboard, this rough-and-ready river port is undergoing a spectacular transformation. Over the past decade, hundreds of towering apartment blocks have sprouted from the city's deep red soil, and new bridges have soared across its muddy river banks. The skyline, a thicket of skyscrapers, already resembles Hong Kong's. Yet the construction frenzy shows no sign of slowing: entering Chongqing is like walking into a giant building site. On the city's northern outskirts, bulldozers flatten wooded hills and lush ravines to satisfy property developers' insatiable appetite for land. Near the airport, teams of construction workers lay track on a new monorail, which will eventually run to nine lines. And at the heart of the old city, wreckers armed with pickaxes hack at a tangle of grimy slums.

Chongqing municipality is often wrongly called the world's largest city. It is actually a mostly rural city-province a little larger than Scotland, with a resident population of 28 million. Around one-quarter of these people live in the city proper, which is rapidly expanding to accommodate an enormous influx of new urban residents. By 2020, planners expect the city's population to top 12 million. A model of central Chongqing at the municipal planning centre shows a sea of skyscrapers and smart residential compounds dappled by green, verdant spaces. Accompanying captions confidently proclaim that six big cities, twenty-five smaller cities and 495 towns will surround the core megacity, 'just as many stars encircling the moon'. In the local government's cosmic view of their city's development, 'A new Chongqing is galloping to the world.'

Amid all this spectacular development, it is easy to miss the poverty on the ground. Urbanization has brought enormous wealth to the city, but the millions of rural migrants who work on building sites, serve in restaurants and rub flesh in massage parlours remain poor. Many new arrivals from the rural counties that surround the metropolis struggle to scratch a living. Not far from the city centre, scrawny men flog pirated porn DVDs from pavements sticky with cooking slop, rows of women sweat at sewing machines in dank basements, and crowds of unemployed migrants gather at an outdoor labour market. On the mossy stone steps that lead down to the Yangtze River, shirtless old men toil under stout bamboo poles laden with heavy wicker panniers, their muscular calves bulging like tennis balls. Chongqing's famous army of 'stick men' are just as much a part of the modern city as rich businessmen sipping cocktails in glitzy bars.

Chongqing's leaders want many more rural people to migrate to the city and other towns within the municipality. They believe that faster urbanization will unlock economic growth and boost rural incomes. Their ambitious goal is to double the municipality's urban population from 10 million in 2010 to 20 million by 2020. This kind of direct promotion of urbanization is new: for the past fifty years or more, China deliberately held back the pace of migration, partly for fear that cities would not be able to cope with a vast influx of migrants. Chongqing's plan jibes with a shift in national policy: China's 12th Five Year Plan, which runs from 2011 to 2015, explicitly calls for more urbanization and supports the emergence of giant megacities. Li Keqiang, the incoming premier, has consistently expressed his support for speedier urbanization nationwide. But policymakers are playing a high-risk game: forced urbanization could dramatically improve millions of lives – or vastly swell the ranks of the urban poor.

Even without explicit central government support, China is already urbanizing faster than expected. In 2011, the country passed a development milestone: for the first time, more than half its citizens lived in towns or cities. The number of people in urban areas jumped to 691 million, taking China's urbanization ratio past 51 per cent. In the development stakes, that puts China many decades behind rich economies like the United Kingdom and the United States, which became predominantly urban countries in 1851 and 1920 respectively. But China's urbanization process is occurring at a mind-boggling rate. In 1980, fewer than 200 million people lived in towns and cities. Over the next thirty years, China's cities expanded by nearly 500 million – the equivalent of adding the combined populations of the USA, the UK, France and Italy.

The primary driving force behind urbanization is economic. Migrant workers earn far more than those who stay on the farm. And the productivity gains from the twin processes of urbanization and industrialization are vital for the national economy: moving hundreds of millions of people out of economically insignificant jobs on the land, and into factories and onto building sites in the city, produces enormous economic growth. Mass migration to the cities makes sense both for individual farmers and for the country as a whole. For this reason, nothing is likely to halt the huge migration from farm to city – bar economic collapse, political turmoil or some other cataclysmic event. Historical experience, economic logic and government policy all point to the same conclusion: by 2030, 1 billion Chinese will live in cities.

This leaves two central questions. What kind of lives will China's urban billion lead? And what will China's cities be like?

China's urbanization numbers are very impressive, but they hide an unpalatable truth: a large chunk of Chinese urbanization is bogus. Up to 250 million people in Chinese cities do not live genuinely urban lives, because migrant workers from the countryside are not entitled to urban social security and face institutionalized discrimination in the cities. China's household registration – or *hukou* – system legally ties migrant workers to their rural home, preventing them from putting down proper roots in the city. Rural migrants in the city lead segregated lives, hidden away in worker dormitories or slum villages. As temporary residents with few legal rights, most migrants remain trapped in low-income jobs, save as much as they can, and buy few goods or services. For this reason, China has failed to reap many of the economic benefits from its huge surge in migration.

The rapid modernization of urban China over the past couple of decades is astonishing, but social stratification is worsening. Without *hukou* reform, China's cities will soon be home to several hundred million second-class citizens. Even the lucky residents who enjoy full urban rights must put up with clogged roads, polluted skies and cityscapes of unremitting ugliness. China is trying hard to make its cities more liveable, but the sheer speed and scale of the urbanization process mean this will be extremely tough to achieve. The problem is made worse by urban planners' impoverished view of modernity, which often requires obliterating the past to make way for the new. China's cities will continue to shock and awe – but they will struggle to inspire hearts and minds.

城市化

For thirty years, China has pursued an exploitative model of urbani-zation that allowed it to industrialize on the cheap. But that model has run its course. As China's cities grow, their biggest challenge is to find a healthier path to urban development. This book aims to show why this must happen and to explain how it can be achieved. First, it describes the process by which hundreds of millions of people will move off the land and into the city. And second, it suggests how China can begin to create liveable cities that fully capture the economic benefits of urbanization.

China's internal migration bears comparison with the great migration from Europe to the USA a century ago. Every year, millions of farmers leave the drudgery of the fields for the bright lights of the cities (see Chapter 1). Most migrants arrive in the city empty-handed, live in squalid conditions and do the dirty work that no one else wants to do. In return, they are denied health care, schooling for their children and basic social security. As more migrant families begin to settle in cities permanently, equitable access to affordable housing and social welfare is becoming a pressing issue. Integrating hundreds of millions of rural migrants into urban society is one of the greatest challenges, both economic and social, that China faces over the next two decades.

A crucial step will be reforming the household registration system (see Chapter 2). Because migrant workers do not have local residence permits, they are treated like illegal immigrants in their own country. Pressure to reform the dispiriting *hukou* system has been growing since the late 1990s, but the central government has failed to make any fundamental changes. New plans to extend an alternative system of local residence permits to migrant workers in cities across China are encouraging. But city governments will struggle financially to provide migrant workers with more urban benefits. If China is serious about delinking social security entitlements from citizens' *hukou* status, the central government will have to bear much more of the financial strain.

Healthier urbanization also requires bold land reforms (see Chapter 3). All rural land is currently owned by village collectives, which do a poor job of protecting individual farmers' rights. Illegal land grabs – when farmers are thrown off their land against their wishes or without proper compensation – are by far the biggest cause of social instability across the country. Ambitious reforms in Chengdu and Chongqing, which allow farmers to sell the use rights to their rural homesteads, are boosting rural incomes and enabling farmers to migrate to cities with cash in their pockets. But they also provide greedy officials and village cadres with an excuse to steal more land. Until collectives are abolished and individual farmers gain private property rights, these abuses will continue and farmers will not begin to capture the true value of their land.

Demand for land is fuelled by China's urban expansion, which is driving the biggest construction boom ever seen (see Chapter 4). The national urban development plan promotes the growth of large cities surrounded by smaller satellites, but local officials will continue to push the development of small cities. This will create a unique pattern of concentrated yet dispersed urbanization. As urban development moves inland, provincial capitals like Chengdu and Wuhan will swell into vast megacities, allowing more rural migrants to find jobs nearer home. The problem of urban sprawl, particularly in the form of new housing developments and vast industrial zones, will get worse so long as China's dysfunctional fiscal system requires cash-strapped local governments to sell land to make ends meet.

China's economic model encourages overinvestment and waste on an enormous scale, but fears that China is a massive bubble are overblown (see Chapter 5). Critics of 'ghost towns' do not appreciate the scale of China's urbanization process: most empty apartment blocks will fill up in time. But China's rapidly growing cities will remain ugly, congested and polluted. Urban planning exists within a closed political system that rewards government officials for promoting economic growth rather than creating a pleasant living environment for residents. The scale of urban development also means that speedy construction trumps aesthetic niceties. The most serious challenge for China's cities is to control the growth of private car ownership and build efficient mass public transit systems – otherwise they risk grinding to a halt.

Chinese leaders hope that the urban investment frenzy will gradually give way to a new model of economic growth fired by household consumption (see Chapter 6). Although excitement about the rural consumer is misplaced, China's long-awaited consumption boom is filtering down to smaller cities. But urban consumption is lower than it should be: if China's leaders are serious about rebalancing the economy, they will need to find the courage to dismantle the legal and social barriers that currently prevent migrant workers from becoming urban consumers. If they do, they could help unleash a huge source of potential demand to drive China's growth in coming decades.

Making urbanization work will require three conditions. First, around 300 million farmers need to move from their villages and into cities. To ensure that farmers are not forced off their land with little compensation, China must abandon the principle of collectively owned land and give farmers secure private property rights. If farmers can rent out or sell their land, they will be able to migrate with a modicum of financial security. China must also reform its discriminatory household registration and residence laws, so that rural migrants enjoy a social safety net when they arrive in the city.

Second, China must build larger, denser, yet more liveable cities. This means creating patterns of urban growth that use resources efficiently and avoid irreversible urban sprawl. Beijing's jammed roads and filthy air show what happens when cities expand around ever-widening ring roads and ever-higher rates of car ownership. Crucially, creating modern, civilized cities will also require building millions of affordable new homes and thousands of hospitals and schools. China's cities will only function as social organisms if they are built to accommodate all urban residents – natives *and* migrants.

Third, China must integrate hundreds of millions of rural migrants into city life. This will probably prove to be the toughest challenge of all. Developing an urban consumer economy will require extending the social welfare system to all urban residents, whether they were born in the city or not, and creating hundreds of millions of new jobs. Since the bulk of China's urban population growth will come from low-income rural migrants, the expansion of the urban population will not magically create a new middle class of consumers.

If China's leaders get urbanization right, they may succeed in tilting the world's second-largest economy away from its reliance on investment and manufacturing towards greater consumption of goods and services. City folk are richer and consume far more than their country cousins. If rural migrants can become genuine consumers, they will rebalance China's economy and put future growth on a more sustainable footing. But if China's leaders get urbanization wrong, the country could spend the next twenty years languishing in middle-income torpor, its cities pockmarked by giant slums. Nearly one in three urban residents do not currently receive urban social benefits, a figure that could climb to nearer one in two if reforms are not made.

Above all, the central government must take some of the financial pressure off local governments by shouldering more of the fiscal burden of reform. How the process of urbanization is financed could decide whether China's current economic model continues, stalls or blows up in its leaders' faces. If China gets urbanization right, it will surpass the United States and cement its position as the world's largest economy. But if it turns sour, the world's most populous country could easily become home to the world's largest urban underclass. That would be a disaster.

1

By the Sweat of Their Brows:
The People Who Built Urban China

For a week or two in late winter or early spring, depending on when the lunar New Year falls, China's cities shut down. Construction halts, shops and restaurants close, and factory gates are bolted. Most urbanites barely notice the millions of rural migrants who live among them until they disappear for the holiday. But without the floating population of migrant workers, who flock to the cities from villages across the country, modern China would not exist. It is no exaggeration to say that these men and women, many barely out of school, power China's urban economy.

Chen Fangyan, who sells fruit on the streets of Beijing, is a typical migrant. Chen's parents moved to Beijing from their village in Henan province in the early 1990s, leaving their young daughter at home in the village. Like tens of millions of left-behind children in China, Chen only saw her parents during the holiday at Chinese New Year. 'I minded a little bit each time my parents returned to the city, but not much,' she says, matter-of-factly. 'After all, there's nothing we could do about it – they had to earn a living.' In 2004, as soon as she finished school, Chen followed her parents to the capital. Now, after eight years in Beijing, she could almost pass for a city girl. But Chen's dyed-brown, semi-frizzed thatch of hair marks her as an outsider: the shaggy-dog look is not popular among fashionable locals.

Chen and her husband share a single room in a squat brick house in northeast Beijing. They live in what is colloquially known as a 'village in the city' – one of an estimated 600 former rural communities in the capital that have been swallowed up by urban sprawl. Only a decade ago, the village was home to farmers growing vegetables. Then the city government bought up the fields for development, compensating villagers with a lump sum and a city *hukou*, giving them the right to live in the city on a legally permanent basis. Villagers used the cash to buy modern flats, and rented out their old homes to migrant workers. Today the bustling streets ring with the dialects of Henan and Anhui, two of the biggest providers of migrant labour in Beijing. A whiff of fetid water hangs over the village, which is dirty, crowded and rundown. But birds sing in the trees, children scamper freely, and the atmosphere is friendly. Nearly 3 million of Beijing's estimated 7 million migrant workers live in urban villages like this.

The village's brick houses are divided into cramped rooms that migrant families rent for around US$80 per month. Chen's 15-square-metre home contains a television, rice cooker and washing machine – exactly what you would find in any modestly prosperous rural home. An urban addition is a cheap computer, which Chen uses to search the Internet for a second-hand fridge. There are few other luxuries: an old iron bedstead is covered in dirty blankets, washing hangs from a wire strung across the room, and electric cables sprout from the wall. A single hot pipe runs from a coal heater, but the room is freezing in winter. Boxes of fruit are stacked against the wall.

Every night at 2 a.m. Chen's husband drives his minivan to a large food wholesale market on the other side of Beijing. Then he drives back and sleeps for an hour or two before setting out for work. Chen stands on the street beside her fruit-laden tricycle for ten hours every day of the week. Many migrant workers have tougher jobs, but

Chen is frequently accosted by city patrol units (*chengguan*) – thugs who clear the streets of vagrants and peddlers, confiscating produce and meting out fines with fists. The fruit business did well in 2010, bringing in nearly US$8,000. But Chen and her husband struggled with rising prices in 2011 as food inflation surged by more than 10 per cent. 'The wholesale costs were really high, but people didn't want to buy expensive fruit,' Chen sighs. 'We save almost all the money we make, but every day there's pressure to make ends meet. You can see it on my husband's face – he's always tired and stressed.'

Like many people from the countryside, Chen and her husband ignored China's one-child rule. They have two boys. Looking after children in the city, where migrant children struggle to find places in state schools, is tough. Chen's younger son boards at a nursery school for migrant children on the outskirts of Beijing, and only comes home at weekends. 'We're too busy working to look after him every day,' Chen says. Her elder son returned to rural Henan to attend primary school, where he can study for free, and her younger son will follow soon. They will stay in the family homestead with their grandfather, who used to live in Beijing but had to leave after contracting tuberculosis. As a migrant worker without access to subsidized health care, he could not afford the cost of treatment in the city.

For migrant workers like Chen, life in China's cities is hard and unfair, and often cold and uncomfortable. Most have no social security, and the feared city patrols may stop them from earning a living. Chen has little contact with local Beijingers, except when they buy a bag of apples or a box of strawberries. This is typical: migrant workers live isolated lives, ghettoized both socially and physically. Yet Chen and her husband, like most young migrants in China's cities, are determined not to go back to rural Henan. They will stay in the city permanently, Chen says, and wait for their sons to join them. 'Locals look down on us because we're poor,' she says. 'But we'll never go back to work the land – we have two children to support!'

城市化

China's great migration from farm to city is only thirty years old. For most of Mao Zedong's rule, freedom of movement between the countryside and the cities was tightly controlled. The Communist Party's revolutionary credentials supposedly lay in the countryside, but its goal was urban industrialization. Protecting the productivity of China's cities, which were viewed primarily as centres of heavy industry, meant limiting inflows of farmers. In the early years of Communist rule there was, in fact, extensive rural-to-urban migration. But that stopped in 1958 with the introduction of the household registration system. The *hukou* system proved a useful tool of social control, but it was originally designed to prevent rural migration to the cities. Farmers had to stay on the farm to produce food to feed urban workers, not move to the cities to gobble it up.

In the 1980s, as Beijing began to loosen its economic and social grip, rural workers were encouraged to 'leave the land but not the villages, enter the factories but not the cities'. The success of township and village enterprises, owned and run by rural collectives, spawned a policy of small-town development. Nationally, the government advocated 'controlling the big cities, moderating the development of medium-sized cities, and encouraging the growth of small cities'. Yet it made an exception in the southern coastal ports of Shenzhen, Zhuhai, Shantou and Xiamen, where the opening of experimental 'special economic zones' began to attract the first trickle of rural migrants into China's cities. By the end of the 1980s, as factories mushroomed along the southeast coast, the number of rural migrants heading for the cities had deepened into a steady stream.

In the early 1990s, migrant flows accelerated again. Global manufacturers moved into China and set up factories all along the coast. Migrant workers were cheap, and jobs were plentiful. Young farmers flocked from their villages to assemble widgets in export-processing factories, to wait tables in new restaurants, and to lug bricks around building sites. Officially, China stuck to its policy of restricting the growth of large cities, even as tens of millions of migrant workers voted with their feet and moved to the swelling coastal metropolises. In the late 1990s, in a foretaste of what would occur in 2008, the Asian financial crisis struck, the economy faltered and exports slumped. As state enterprises began to lay off millions of urban workers, new job opportunities for rural migrants dwindled.

In the early years of the new century the economy recovered, exports boomed and China's urban property market exploded. As the demand for labour grew, the stream of rural migrants swelled into a flood, leaving the cities awash with new residents. During the first decade of the new century, nearly 100 million new rural migrants flocked to China's cities to find work, and urban policy finally shifted to recognize the reality on the ground. The 11th Five Year Plan (2006–10) advocated 'balanced development' of cities, regardless of size. The 12th Five Year Plan (2011–15) went further, explicitly promoting the growth of metropolitan regions and urban clusters of large cities orbited by smaller satellites. Current leaders are enthusiastically pro-urban: there is a consensus that developing prosperous cities is the key to fostering greater domestic demand.

After thirty years of expansion, China's migrant labour flows have become so large that they are almost impossible to count. China's urban population data are more accurate. They tell us that the number of people resident for six months or more in China's cities grew by more than 200 million in the first decade of the century, the equivalent of adding the population of Australia every year. Nearly half of this increase came from rural-to-urban migration. Today, surveys indicate that around 160 million rural migrants work in cities far from home, more than the population of Russia. A further 60 million migrants have left their villages to live in local towns and cities, while another 35 million semi-migrants work at non-agricultural jobs during the day, returning home to their villages only to sleep. According to a government forecast, a further 250 million rural residents will migrate to cities by 2030, accounting for more than two-thirds of the projected increase in China's urban population. The remainder will come from natural population growth and from the reclassification of rural residents as urban.

Rural migrants can be divided into two broad categories. The first are traditional migrant workers – the so-called 'floating population' (*liudong renkou*) of rural muscle who move to the city on a supposedly temporary basis. This includes about 220 million migrant workers who live away from their villages. The second category includes the growing millions of farmers who agree, or are forced, to give up their homesteads and land in exchange for a new urban life. This type of migrant is likely to become more common as local governments push through land reforms and attempt to speed up urbanization.

A third, fuzzier category is formed by rural residents who find themselves reclassified as urban citizens. These people can become 'urban' overnight, as rural–urban boundaries are adjusted. Some continue to live much as before, but others have to move out of their rural homes when their village is swallowed by the encroaching city. They may then move into urban apartments in a different part of the city, effectively becoming local migrants themselves. In recent years, rising compensation for requisitioned land on the urban fringe has allowed a growing band of lucky former farmers to grow rich – much to the irritation of grumbling local urbanites. Reclassified urbanites were a big part of the urbanization story over the past fifteen years, but tighter limits on requisitioning farmland for urban development mean they should have a smaller role to play in future.

Around one-third of China's migrants currently cross provincial borders in search of work. Most come from inland China and travel east to the prosperous cities along or near the coast. In the export processing centres of Guangdong, the so-called workshop of the world, migrant workers have long outnumbered local residents. The couple of dozen towns that comprise Dongguan, probably the single biggest magnet for migrant workers nationwide, are dominated by factories and dormitories. Two-thirds of migrant workers are employed in coastal provinces. The 2010 census found that

Guangdong remains a popular destination, sucking in nearly one in three migrants who cross provincial borders. Yet more migrants now find work in the greater Yangtze River Delta region around Shanghai, where there are more jobs and wages are often higher. A far smaller, but still significant, stream of migrant workers head north to Beijing and Tianjin.

The overwhelming majority of migrant workers who cross provincial borders come from just six provinces: Anhui, Guizhou, Henan, Hubei, Hunan and Sichuan. As long as wages are higher on the coast, poorer provinces in the interior will remain net exporters of labour. Take Sichuan, where more than 20 million rural folk have left their villages in search of more lucrative employment. Half of these migrants work in local cities, with up to 2 million gathering in Chengdu alone. But most of the rest work on the east coast, mainly in the Yangtze and Pearl River Deltas. 'If all the migrant workers came home, we wouldn't have enough jobs for them,' says Professor Guo Xiaoming of the Sichuan Academy of Social Sciences in Chengdu.

But migrant flows are beginning to shift. Two-thirds of all migrant workers who travel beyond local towns and cities now find jobs in their home province, and rapidly growing inland cities like Chengdu are attracting far more migrant labour than they did a decade ago. The development of other big inland cities such as Chongqing, Wuhan, Xi'an and Zhengzhou means that many migrant workers now have the opportunity to find work nearer home. In 2011, for the first time, more migrant workers in Henan found jobs within the province than outside it. Migrant flows to inland cities will grow, too, as local farmers swap their land for urban *hukou*. Chongqing, for example, plans to move 7 million farmers into towns and cities between 2012 and 2020 in exchange for urban housing and social welfare. The big cities on the east coast are still growing quickly, but the urbanization process over the next two decades will be much more evenly balanced between the coast and the interior.

There is one important caveat to this analysis: migrant flows are not set in stone. China's migrant workers are among the most flexible in the world and will quickly move to wherever the work is – but migrants will go nowhere if there are no jobs for them. When export factories in the Pearl River Delta began to shed workers in late 2008 after the onset of the global financial crisis, millions of migrant workers headed home early for Chinese New Year. An estimated 23 million failed to return, either sitting out the downturn on the farm or picking up jobs closer to home, often on infrastructure projects created by China's massive economic stimulus programme. This reversed the steady stream of migrant labour from west to east, which had continued unabated for nearly three decades. In 2009, the number of migrants who left their home area to work in coastal cities dropped by 9 per cent to 91 million, while those in central and western provinces jumped 35 per cent, to 54 million.

This is a cautionary lesson for bullish China watchers who believe that mass migration will underpin economic growth for the next twenty or more years. The fact that China is still far less urbanized than most developed countries does not guarantee that China will catch up. Urbanization *will* underpin economic growth for many years to come *if* China's economy continues to create enough jobs to absorb millions of extra workers. For the moment, many export businesses in the Pearl River Delta complain that there are not enough migrants to fill factory floors. But if a global economic crash destroyed China's export machine, for example, then the greatest human migration in history could falter – or even go into reverse.

城市化

Migrant workers are known colloquially as the 'floating population' because they drift from place to place without putting down urban roots. These people are among the most enterprising of China's vast, rural-born populace, but they must battle against institutional barriers designed to prevent them from becoming permanent urban citizens. Under China's household registration system, most city governments only provide public welfare and social security to residents with a local urban residence permit, the *hukou*. Few migrant workers enjoy subsidized local health care and most pay for their children's schooling. If they lose their job, they will probably receive no unemployment benefit and may have to return to the countryside.

The older generation of rural migrants – defined as those born before 1980 – are guest workers in their own country. They live in China's cities temporarily, and plan to return home when they grow old. The majority of these workers regard themselves as rural and have little or no desire to change their rural status. But this traditional pattern of migration is changing. Surveys show that the majority of the new generation of migrant workers – those born after 1980 – have no intention of returning to the penury of rural life. They are significantly better educated than their parents and usually adapt far more quickly to urban ways. They hope to become fully fledged urban citizens and enjoy a modern consumer lifestyle. Many of them have never tilled a field in their lives. Yet, thanks to China's discriminatory household registration system, these urban wannabes find themselves shut out of urban society.

In 2009, the National Bureau of Statistics (NBS) surveyed 68,000 rural households across thirty-one provinces and a further 6,000 'new generation' migrants in ten provinces. The surveys showed that migrant workers are getting younger: 60 per cent of those who found work far from home were born in the 1980s or 1990s. A full half of the rural-registered population aged under 30 worked in towns and cities. On average, the new generation of migrants left home aged 20, falling to just 17 for those born in the 1990s. They are the first generation to be 'non-agricultural': 90 per cent did not spend a single day in the fields. By comparison, some 30 per cent of older generation migrant workers did some agricultural work, such as collecting in the harvest, during the previous year. This is significant: the fact that the vast majority of young migrant workers do not understand farming means they are far less likely than their parents to return to the countryside.

Nearly half of all young migrants work in manufacturing, particularly in coastal provinces such as Guangdong and Zhejiang. A large number are young women, who are favoured for their diligence and deft fingers. Other young migrants seek jobs in the service sector, delivering goods, serving in restaurants or cleaning apartments. They view these jobs as preferable to the more physically demanding construction work favoured by older, male migrants. Professor Guo at the Sichuan Academy of Social Sciences says younger migrants' unwillingness to put up with poor working conditions shows up in migrant flow statistics. The proportion of Sichuanese working in the Pearl River Delta dropped substantially in 2009 as younger migrants went elsewhere in search of better pay and conditions.

Still, millions of migrants of all ages end up working in dangerous or unpleasant conditions. Prostitution is rife in China's cities, and the vast majority of women who work as massage girls in barber shops and bathhouses are from the countryside. Beautiful women who accompany rich businessmen in karaoke parlours can easily make US$3,000 per month, and some find this work preferable to the hard grind of an ordinary migrant job. But the most desperate female migrants work from stained beds in dark basements, charging as little as US$2 to service their male counterparts, who probably only see their wives for a week or two at Chinese New Year. Migrant workers also live at the whim of their bosses, who may withhold wages or refuse to allow days off. Their weak legal position means that employer abuses often go unpunished.

Nothing better illustrates migrant workers' second-class status than their living conditions. Almost all urban natives today live in modern housing units with private kitchens and bathrooms. But this is an unheard-of luxury for the vast majority of rural migrants. Two-thirds sleep in company dormitories or temporary housing on building sites – sometimes in prefabricated huts, but often in large canvas tents – or simply curl up on the shop floor. Those migrants who settle in the city typically rent private bedsits in rundown urban villages or dingy basements, where they buy fewer goods and services than settled urbanites. Migrant workers spend less than urban natives because they have less cash, but also because they tend to live in temporary accommodation far from modern urban markets. The vast majority of rural migrants working in cities remain only partially urbanized: they may live in the city, but most are not economically active participants in urban life.

Visitors to China puzzle how its cities appear to have passed through the messy business of industrialization without developing the miserable street poverty found in other developing cities. In Delhi, a new slum pops up with every new shopping mall. How have large Chinese cities like Tianjin and Guangzhou avoided this? Contrary to government propaganda, China *does* have slums. But China's slums do not look like the large makeshift cities and shanty towns that house the urban poor in many other countries. Many are former villages, like Cheng Fangyan's, that have been gobbled up by the expanding city. Other slums are decrepit neighbourhoods of old urban housing known as 'shanty areas'. Once home to farmers or working-class urbanites, these run-down urban neighbourhoods house anywhere between one-quarter and one-half of China's migrant workers.

In northern China, urban slum villages are typically shabby clusters of squat, brick homes. In some southern cities, such as Kunming, they are a mishmash of taller, concrete structures with shoddy new floors built by opportunistic landlords. They are typically overcrowded, lacking proper sanitation. Yet they hardly compare to the huge, festering slums that blight cities in India and Africa. China has avoided this fate thanks to its authoritarian political system, which gives local governments a much higher degree of control over migrant flows and housing than governments have in other countries. Central to the state's web of social control is the *hukou* system, which ties all citizens and most entitlements to social welfare to their place of registration – normally the place of their parents' birth. Because schooling is hard to find and health care is expensive, migrant workers traditionally leave their families in the countryside. And because migrant workers generally retain their rural homes, they can return if they do not find a job.

Hukou restrictions have relaxed significantly since economic reforms began in the 1980s, but they still act as a barrier to permanent migration. Compare this to India, where freedom of movement is enshrined in the constitution, enabling whole rural families to move to the city at will. India's policy has its own problems: it is easier for rural migrants to swap a life of penury in the countryside for a squalid life in the city. But in China, those migrant workers who do attempt to create a genuine urban life for themselves are effectively sequestered out of sight and, many would argue, out of mind. They live in slum villages or in basements, in accommodation that is effectively sanctioned by local officials. When those same officials decide that an urban slum has become unsightly or they determine to sell the land for development, they simply clear the migrants out.

This system has its advantages: China's rural migrants live less squalid lives than many of their counterparts in other countries. The vast majority have access to clean water and proper (if often filthy) lavatories, few sleep on the street, and hardly any die of cholera. Because China restricts the migration of rural households, its cities have coped with the influx of migrants better than those in most other developing countries. Notably, China's cities do not swarm with malnourished street children. But this success comes at the cost of freedom of movement and hindered social mobility: it is a system of urban development built on repression and violence.

The system cannot continue indefinitely. The major reason is the changing profile of the migrant population: the new generation of migrant workers increasingly want to settle in the cities permanently, and they want their families to join them. If NBS's survey is accurate, a full two-thirds of migrants now arrive in the city with at least some members of their family in tow. China's *hukou* system no longer restricts mobility as it once did. As the number of rural migrants in China's cities grows, they will struggle to find cheap housing – especially as Chinese cities continue their policy of demolishing urban slum villages. Where will migrant workers go when their homes are destroyed? Either a growing number of migrants will have to crowd into ever smaller city slums and basements, or shanty towns will begin to pop up on the edges of cities. For China's leaders, the choice is stark: extend urban welfare, including modern subsidized housing, to migrant workers, or accept a proliferation of slums as the inevitable price of development.

城市化

For migrant workers, the lack of affordable housing, education and health care in China's cities are by far the biggest obstacles to permanent migration. Many farming families still live basically subsistence lives, eating vegetables grown on the family plot. Most of the income they earn from selling crops or meat is spent on food, clothing and building materials. Life in the city is much more expensive: migrant workers have to pay rent, move around the city, and buy food. Current *hukou* policy exacerbates the problem, because rural migrants' lack of social insurance makes life in the city even more costly. Many migrant parents send their children back to the village when they reach school age, because they cannot afford private schooling in the city. Unsurprisingly, studies show that 'left-behind children' frequently suffer psychological trauma and perform worse than their peers at school. Many villages in China today are populated mainly by children and their grandparents, as everyone of working age has left for the cities.

Rural migrants earn considerably less than urban natives. The average monthly salary for migrant workers was a little over Rmb2,000 (about US$325) in 2011, according to a survey by the Ministry of Human Resources and Social Security. Migrant wages have risen rapidly in recent years, but they still fall far short of the national average wage, which is in excess of Rmb3,200 (US$510). Migrant workers also work harder. NBS surveys indicate that the average migrant works nine hours a day, six days a week; overtime is standard in many jobs. Rural migrants typically have no urban assets and remain far poorer than residents with urban *hukou*. Yet some earn as much in a month as farmers back home earn in a year – so the financial benefits of migration justify the hardship.

Over the next two decades, China must find a way of integrating hundreds of millions of rural migrants into urban society. New policies are needed to enable migrant workers to settle permanently in urban society, from building more public housing to reforming China's discriminatory household registration system. The immediate challenge is to ensure that migrant workers' children are allowed to attend state-funded schools, and families have somewhere decent to live. Even for the 40 per cent of migrants who move off the construction site or shop floor and into private digs, living conditions are generally awful. Migrant workers commonly live in poky, shared rooms with barely enough room for a bed. Only one-fifth of migrant workers have access to their own kitchen and lavatory.

The obvious solution is for local governments to build more public rental housing to accommodate migrant workers. In 2011, the central government decreed that China would build 36 million units of 'social' housing over five years, including millions of public rental units. Its goal is for 20 per cent of the urban population to live in some form of subsidized housing by 2015. But there are considerable doubts over whether the government will hit its targets and how this building will be financed. Rosealea Yao, a property analyst at GK Dragonomics in Beijing, reckons the official target includes all sorts of housing that is not genuinely 'social'. She estimates that the actual net increase in new housing supply will total about 20 million units once you strip out a large chunk of non-market housing, such as university dormitories, that would have been built anyway.

Moreover, in many cities, tight controls on who moves into social housing mean that most units will be snapped up by urban natives, not migrant workers. There is little motive for local governments to provide housing for outsiders, especially when locals on low incomes complain they cannot afford to buy housing at market rates. Even in those cities where a local *hukou* is not required to access social housing, prospective occupants are required to provide a pile of paperwork to prove that they are long-term residents and financially secure. Migrant workers without proof of stable employment and a history of social insurance contributions will miss out.

Nevertheless, some lucky migrants will make the cut. One of the first examples of a large public rental housing scheme that accepts migrant workers is the People's Heart Park in Chongqing. The complex's 70,000 residents are a mixture of working-class urbanites, young people looking for cheap accommodation, and long-term migrant workers from Chongqing's rural counties. The thirty-storey tower blocks appear hastily built, but have guards at their entrances, underground car parks, tree-lined walkways and children's playgrounds. They look identical to typical market housing, but contain smaller units. Rent in 2011 was Rmb11 per square metre per month, which worked out as roughly US$80 per month for a standard apartment. The complex, which is surrounded by dozens of other new developments, has a convenient bus service into the city centre and its own monorail station.

People's Heart Park is a rare example of a government policy that enables rural migrants and urban natives to live side by side. One middle-aged woman fetching her clothes from the complex's launderette says she moved from her old apartment in central Chongqing because she could rent a larger, newer apartment in People's Heart Park for the same price. 'There are lots of migrants living here, but that's not a problem,' she says. 'No one looks down on country folk any more.'

But most migrants tell a different story. City natives rarely talk to migrant workers, unless they are being served by one. It is easy to spot migrant outsiders, who tend to be unmannered in metropolitan ways. In Chongqing's main shopping district, rheumy-eyed old men dressed in rolled-up trousers and flimsy plimsolls gaze at rich locals shopping in luxury stores. Ungainly women from the countryside, attempting to look sophisticated, hoof along the street in shiny hot pants and cheap nylons. Many rural people struggle to find their way in urban society.

Zhu Yi, a social scientist who studies personal well-being, runs an NGO that helps migrant workers in Chongqing integrate into urban society. Classes provide practical information about how to access social insurance and government training programmes. But they also aim to boost rural migrants' self-confidence. 'When migrants move to the city they encounter a disorienting environment and culture. They feel lower than city folk, who often look down on them, and ashamed of their rural identity,' she explains. 'We aim to change how they think about themselves.'

Migrant workers struggle to adapt to urban life for a number of social, cultural and economic reasons. But the sense of inferiority felt by many rural folk is institutionalized by the *hukou* system, which clearly divides the country between haves and have-nots. China spends far more on its urban citizens than on its rural citizens, even when those rural citizens live and work in the city. The division is so brutal that critics have labelled the system 'China's apartheid'. As long as China maintains this system, much of its vaunted urbanization will remain essentially bogus. For migrant workers to have a decent chance of a better future, China must reform its pernicious *hukou* system.

BOX 1.1   Beijing's slum clearances

Until it was demolished in 2010, Bajiacun in northeast Beijing was just one of hundreds of run-down urban 'villages' housing the city's poor. Hidden away on the northern edge of the capital's university district, just a few hundred yards east of the prestigious Tsinghua campus, Bajiacun's dilapidated streets were home to a small core of working-class Beijingers and thousands of migrant workers renting cheap lodgings. Once the demolition crew had left, all that remained of the once teeming village were several hectares of cleared land and a handful of trees, standing starkly amid a grey and dusty expanse of flattened rubble. 'Every village must push ahead with urbanization to create a better tomorrow,' proclaimed a painted slogan at the edge of the demolition site.

At the beginning of 2010, Beijing officials identified 677 villages within or on the fringes of the city's urban borders, which they estimated were home to 630,000 permanent local residents and some 2.8 million migrants. Bajiacun, whose name literally means 'Eight House Village', was one of fifty villages picked by the city government for demolition in 2010 under a plan to integrate Beijing's former rural communities into the city's urban fabric. Razing the fifty villages will free up 25 square kilometres of land on which to build modern apartment blocks. Under the plan, all permanent local residents – who collectively own the land on which the village is built – will be temporarily rehoused for a couple of years before being resettled in a new flat near their old home. The urbanized villagers, most of whom retain their traditional rural residence status, will then be entitled to transfer to an urban *hukou*. Rural migrants are expected to rent new apartments built on top of the old village, with some of the income being shared among the members of the former village collective.

Beijing's demolition and resettlement project bears similarities to schemes in Europe and North America before and after World War II. Like the London slum clearances of the 1930s, Beijing's scheme is designed to tear down old, substandard housing occupied by the urban poor and replace them with modern homes. 'Slum' is a loaded word that needs to be used with care: Beijing's villages are neither the tuberculosis-ridden rookeries of Dickens's London nor the cholera-filled shanty towns of modern Mumbai. They are neither sordid nor disease-ridden. But they are overcrowded and shoddily constructed; they enjoy few public services or amenities; and the narrow, rubbish-strewn streets and alleyways quickly flood when the summer rains arrive. Rooms are typically poky and cold, with low ceilings and little natural light. Villagers share communal outdoor lavatories – iceboxes in winter – squatting side by side in unpartitioned rows of three.

Beijing's plan to transform the city's villages into modern urban districts has both social and economic motives. It is primarily designed to provide decent living conditions for working-class locals and new rental units for migrant workers, who flock to the capital from every corner of China. And it is designed to promote urbanization and integrate the bottom rung of society into the urban economy.

One of the largest villages to be demolished was Tangjialing, whose squalid streets on the northern fringe of the city were home to more than 50,000 graduate 'ants' – young white-collar workers and unemployed youths unable to afford decent accommodation elsewhere. The district government tore down the area in the summer of 2010, promising to replace the tangled streets and crowded doss-houses with 100,000 square metres of new public rental properties. The local residents who made a living by renting out their old homes in the village will supposedly retain their land-use rights and take a share of the new rental income. Yet assuming each lodger rents a 10-square-metre space, the rented housing would accommodate no more than one-fifth of the previous 50,000 slum residents – so it is far from a complete solution.

Bajiacun's demolition and resettlement project is similar to Tangjialing's. Beijing is testing urban relocation and integration models that set compensation significantly above national standards and are designed to provide a sustainable means of income for local residents. It does this in the hope of avoiding the social unrest associated with land seizures and forced demolitions, when residents are thrown out of their homes. Any trouble of this kind will, of course, be dealt with in China's typically forthright manner. 'Severely smash behaviour that disturbs order during the demolition and resettlement process' warn banners strung up along the perimeter fence at Bajiacun. The resettlement model varies from village to village, but locals say that permanent residents of Bajiacun were each given a sizeable lump sum as compensation for their demolished property. They can then use this to buy a modern 'resettlement apartment' when the developers move out. Ground-floor commercial space is expected to be reserved for locally run shops, restaurants and small businesses, and resettled residents will be encouraged to rent out rooms to migrants.

A few hundred yards north of the Bajiacun demolition site, new blocks of resettlement flats are springing up. On posters showing gleaming 23–27-storey tenements surrounded by green spaces, slogans push the government line on urban integration: 'Share in the real life of the capital!' The idyllic images are in marked contrast to the sprawling warren of village slum housing that survives to the east and the north of the building site. Stray dogs sniff at streets littered with plastic wrappers; mangy hens pick at kitchen slop; washing hangs by the roadside. The walls in the dingy alleyways are papered with cheaply printed advertisements offering casual work. Street stalls sell snacks from Sichuan, a major source of migrant labour.

These streets are slated for demolition, too, although no one knows when that will be. They house some of the former migrant residents of Bajiacun, who moved up the road when the wreckers tore down their old lodgings. Mrs Shu, a native of rural Chengdu, shared a 10-square-metre room with her two children in Bajiacun for more than a decade, for which she paid around US$30 per month. She now rents a room for US$80 and cannot afford to pay more. Mr Liu, a migrant worker from Anhui province, is in a similar position. 'I won't be able to afford the rent in the new apartments when they're built, so I'll have to find a cheap room in a village further out of town,' he says. In theory, cheap rental housing will be available to non-local *hukou* holders like Mrs Shu and Mr Liu – but huge questions remain over both the volume and its affordability. Whether these homes are truly accessible to the migrant poor will determine whether Beijing's urban integration programme is a success or a failure.

28   CHINA'S URBAN BILLION

BOX 1.2   School's out

In August 2011, the Beijing municipal government ordered the demolition of 24 unauthorized schools attended by the children of migrant workers, just days before the new school year was due to start. The local authorities said 14,000 children were affected (although some reports put the figure nearer 30,000) and that the closures were needed to protect children from unsafe buildings and poor teaching. But the decision caused outrage among migrants and local residents alike, who accused the city government of trampling on migrant workers' rights. Both views contain elements of truth.

Ministry of Education guidelines state that all local authorities have a duty to provide nine years of free schooling to migrant children, but a large proportion of migrant children fail to find a place in state primary and middle schools. Government surveys show that slightly over half of migrant workers' children go home for their education, usually living with their grandparents. Of those who remain in the city, 80 per cent find places at state schools, while 20 per cent are educated in private schools set up for migrant children. If these figures are correct, fewer than 40 per cent of migrant workers' children are educated in state schools in their parents' place of work.

More than one-third of Beijing's 20 million inhabitants are rural migrants, and the capital is home to nearly half a million migrant children of compulsory school age. According to the local education authority, 70 per cent of these children are educated in state schools. Around 100,000 attend private schools for migrants, roughly split between those attending schools authorized by the education bureau and those attending unauthorized – and therefore illegal – schools.

Beijing allows migrant children to attend state schools if their parents provide five separate documents proving their local employment and temporary residence status. In practice, parents can also buy their way into the state system by paying a 'sponsorship' fee, often in addition to tuition fees. But few migrants are able to provide the necessary paperwork, and fewer still can afford to pay extra fees. Some schools waive the requirements and allow migrant children to study anyway, but other children are expected to return to their rural 'home' to study (even if they were born in the city).

Beijing's district authorities say they plan to close all unauthorized schools in the city. In addition to the 24 schools demolished in the summer of 2011, 114 other private schools are classed as illegal. The better schools may obtain the necessary licence and remain open, but others face the wrecking ball. Officials are right to point out that some of these unauthorized schools do not meet minimum standards and are profiteering. Thousands of children study in shoddy buildings under unqualified teachers. But schools may be closed for other reasons – because the local government wants to sell the land for development or, most likely, because its education budget is overstretched. Above all, officials fear that opening up all state schools will encourage more migrant workers to bring their children to the city, crippling the local education system.

Despite the negative headlines, the situation in Beijing probably has not deteriorated in recent years. Migrant workers have always struggled to find affordable schooling; that is why so many send their children home. And the fact that a growing number of migrants are accompanied by their children suggests the situation may even be improving. Take Xinzhuang, a migrant slum village in east Beijing. Long-term residents say that until 2008 their children were unable to attend local state schools; but since then some children have gone to class with native Beijingers. Other parents, whose children attended unauthorized private schools, panicked when these schools were demolished. But the local authority quickly opened a new school, conveniently located on the edge of the village.

In fact, demographic shifts in China's cities mean that the schooling situation for migrant children is likely to improve. Thanks to China's one-child rule, which is more strictly enforced in cities, native urban populations are ageing rapidly. The result is that thousands of school and millions of teachers will have to be laid off, unless new children can be found to fill empty schools. The obvious solution is to extend education to migrant children. Before long, China's schools could be filled with 'immigrant' children, much as inner-city schools are in many Western countries today.

For the moment, China's record of schooling migrant children is patchy. Other cities have more progressive policies than Beijing; Shanghai, for example, has opened many of its primary and middle schools to children without local *hukou*. But millions of migrant children across China miss out on state education. Even the lucky minority who do go to urban state schools until the age of 15 must then return to the countryside to take their high-school exams. China's report card? Must do better.

2

Passport to Purgatory:
Fixing the *Hukou* System

When farmers leave Chongqing's rural counties to seek work in the city, many end up in the teeming slums of Eighteen Steps. Most of the buildings that now house migrant workers date back to the late 1930s and early 1940s, when China's leader Chiang Kai-shek made the foggy city on the Yangtze his capital during the War of Resistance against Japan. Chungking, as it was known in the West, was deemed far enough inland to be safe from the marauding soldiers of Japan's imperial army. But the wartime capital soon became a major target for Japanese bombers. In 1939, more than 5,000 civilians died during two nights of devastating air raids.

Eighteen Steps is just a ten-minute stroll from the People's Liberation Monument in the heart of the city's commercial and business district. The stone column was built in 1945 to commemorate victory over the Japanese, but in 1950 was declared a monument to the Communist triumph over Chiang Kai-shek's nationalist Kuomintang in China's civil war. Today the column is ringed with foreign luxury stores, evidence of the enormous urban wealth generated over the past decade. But there is little prosperity in the warren of dark buildings that cling to the hillside above the river. The dripping alleyways are lined with dank, squalid houses patched with filthy tarpaulin. Porters ferrying heavy bags up the steep stone steps wheeze past women scrubbing woks in blackened kitchens.

Down the hill, at Nanjimen labour market, a raucous crowd of migrant workers gather daily to look for work. Most of the migrants hail from rural Chongqing, but some travel from the neighbouring provinces of Sichuan and Hubei. They hold pieces of paper scrawled with self-advertisements: 'cook', 'builder', 'delivery man'. Finding a poorly paid job is not hard, they say, but finding a boss who pays a fair wage on time is much tougher. 'All bosses are liars,' says a short man named Xu. 'But the biggest liar of all is the government.' Zhong, a Sichuan native who suffers from badly flaking skin, agrees. 'The government promises much, but it's all empty words,' he says. 'We live in the city, but we do not feel urban. We have no proper home, and no social security.' He points at a bearded man with glassy eyes and a crazed expression slumped on the pavement. 'These people come to the city and cannot find work,' he explains, shaking his head. 'They sleep on the street, and when the pressure becomes too much, they slowly go mad.'

Zhong and Xu share a windowless concrete cell in Eighteen Steps with four other migrant workers. Inside, a man with crippled legs lies on a bed fashioned out of bamboo poles and heavy cotton blankets. Cheap suitcases and nylon-thread bags are stacked on a ledge above his head. The only object of value in the room is a single rice cooker. Outside, a crude, hand-written sign hangs from a stick, advertising beds for Rmb3 per night, about 40 cents. Lodgers walk through a brick entrance past a pile of empty bottles, cardboard boxes and other scrap, which the proprietor collects and sells for change. Rats are common companions. Similar areas in Chongqing have been demolished over the past few years, and Eighteen Steps is due to meet the wreckers' pickaxe: demolition in China is typically done by hand.

The migrant workers in Eighteen Steps live at the bottom of the urban heap. Officially classed as temporary residents, they lead temporary lives, never putting down permanent roots in the city.

Chongqing is engaged in perhaps the most radical experiment in *hukou* reform nationwide, but these men have yet to qualify, even though they have lived in the city for several years. Under the initial reforms, only long-term migrant workers with stable jobs and accommodation can convert to a local urban *hukou*. So they live in the city, but with little access to public services or social welfare. 'I won't go home because I'm not used to the life there anymore,' says Yang, a young migrant worker with hedgehog hair who was born in neighbouring Fengdu county. 'I don't belong in the countryside and I don't belong in the city.'

城市化

East Asian societies have used systems of household registration for hundreds of years, and family registers are still maintained in Taiwan (*hukou*), Japan (*koseki*), North Korea (*hoju*) and Vietnam (*ho khau*). Household registration systems were traditionally used to keep basic administrative tabs on residents, similar to identity-card schemes. But when China introduced its modern household registration system in 1958, it combined elements of the traditional *hukou* with a repressive, Soviet-style internal passport system. Modern household registration – which classifies citizens as either 'rural' or 'non-rural', and ties individuals' right to public welfare to their official place of residence – was originally designed to keep rural residents working on the farm and limit their welfare entitlements. The peculiarly draconian nature of the system crystallized during the famines of the 1960s, when it was necessary to keep a tight lid on the number of urban (officially 'non-rural') *hukou* holders, who were entitled to grain rations.

Originally, the *hukou* system split society into two clearly defined segments: urban and rural. The urban minority enjoyed housing, employment, health care, schooling and food rations, mostly provided by their state work units. The rural majority struggled along with few social benefits, relying on their land for sustenance and security. This simple, if harsh, system began to break down in the

1980s following the decollectivization of agriculture. As migration controls relaxed, the *hukou* system gradually ceased to function as a major deterrent to mobility. Today, at least 220 million Chinese live outside their place of household registration. But the *hukou* system continues to regulate citizens' access to social benefits and public services. Rural migrants are allowed to work in cities on a temporary basis, but most are denied access to health care, utilities subsidies, housing benefits and, in many cases, schooling for their children.

The majority of China's vast army of rural migrants have little chance of securing a local urban *hukou*. They belong to a distinct social group that is neither truly rural nor truly urban. The *hukou* system may no longer be an impenetrable bulwark to movement, but it remains a highly effective class barrier, firmly dividing the urban haves from the rural have-nots. Kam Wing Chan, a professor at the University of Washington in Seattle and an expert on China's household registration system, says the discriminatory system produces 'cities with invisible walls': migrant workers may live *in* the city, but they are not *of* the city. The *hukou* system, he argues, 'is a major source of injustice and inequality, perhaps the most crucial foundation of China's social and spatial stratification, and arguably contributes to the country's most prevalent human rights violations' (Chan et al. 2008: 583).

Since migrant workers are viewed as temporary residents who can always return to their rural homes, local governments and employers rarely treat them in the same way as local citizens. Under China's Labour Contract Law, which was introduced in 2008, migrant workers with formal employment contracts are entitled to certain social protections and entitlements. But these laws are rarely enforced. In any case, the vast majority of migrant workers are employed informally. As low-status outsiders, they are treated as economic cannon fodder. The central government has instructed local authorities to do a better job of providing health care and schooling for migrants, but there is no coordinated national effort to solve the problem. Generally, city governments spend the minimum needed to prevent social instability.

The inhumanity of the current system is plain to see: migrant workers do all the toughest, dirtiest jobs, but receive the smallest social benefits from their work. It is clearly absurd to insist that hundreds of millions of migrant workers remain legally 'rural' when many have lived in cities for years. But excluding migrants from the urban benefits system serves a useful economic function: for thirty years the *hukou* system has effectively allowed China to industrialize on the cheap. The so-called 'China price', which for years allowed China to manufacture and export goods more cheaply than anywhere else, was rooted in a seemingly endless pool of cut-price migrant labour. As Chan puts it, 'Migrant workers without urban *hukou* have become the most important human cog powering the China economic machine' (Chan 2012: 68). The first step to *hukou* reform will be convincing government officials that there is an economic, as well as a social, case for change.

城市化

For the first four decades of the modern *hukou* system, the central government retained control over household registration and population movements. Urban social welfare was financed from central coffers, and Beijing decided which rural *hukou* holders would be allowed to transfer to urban *hukou*. The quota was very tight, and there were only a few possible routes an ambitious farmer could take – for example, by joining the army and being demobilized as an urban citizen, or by securing a rare job as a worker in a state enterprise. Because individual mobility was so limited, the key distinction made by the *hukou* system was simply between 'rural' and 'urban', as very few people lived away from their place of household registration.

This situation changed in the late 1990s when, as part of wider governance reforms, the central government palmed off responsibility for *hukou* controls to local governments. Since then, admission requirements for transferring to urban *hukou* have been determined locally, meaning that the key distinction between different types of *hukou* today is less about 'rural' and 'urban' than it is about local *hukou* and non-local *hukou*. Long-term residents in a particular city are only entitled to all social services – education, health care, social security – if they hold a local urban *hukou*. Both rural migrants and urban residents who move away from their official place of residence have to pay extra to use local city services. As well as dissuading rural migrant workers from bringing their families with them to the city, the lack of a local *hukou* can discourage skilled urban workers and professionals from seeking work away from their home towns.

In 1998, the State Council – China's cabinet – approved a proposal by the Ministry of Public Security (MPS) to remove a number of restrictions on internal migration. The new rules allowed local governments to approve *hukou* conversions for spouses previously separated by different household registrations and allowed under-18s to inherit their *hukou* status from either parent (rather than from only their mother, as had previously been the case). To boost investment in China's cities, local authorities were told to facilitate the transfer of urban *hukou* for incoming investors, professionals and their family members. The reforms made it easier for urban residents to transfer their *hukou* between urban administrations and, supposedly, for skilled rural migrants to register as urban residents.

One of the most ambitious early reformers was Shijiazhuang, the dusty capital of the northern province of Hebei. Shijiazhuang began its reforms in earnest in 2001, determining to boost its relatively poor economic performance both by attracting talented outsiders and by granting local *hukou* to the thousands of rural migrants who had made their home in the city. The city authorities identified eight types of people for whom residency restrictions should be relaxed, including teachers, businessmen, investors and university graduates. Unusually, it added an extra category: rural migrants. The only stipulation was that migrants must have lived and worked in the city for two full years. An excited report in the *China Youth Daily* declared that Shijiazhuang's experiment would 'demolish' the barriers of household registration and provide a 'revolutionary model' for the rest of the country to follow.

The reforms in Shijiazhuang went further than those in most other large cities; but the reality on the ground did not match the media rhetoric. Reports of how many migrant workers took up Shijiazhuang's offer of urban residency vary wildly, between 11,000 and 70,000 in the first year, although some reports claimed that 300,000 migrants would benefit. What is clear is that Shijiazhuang's *hukou* reforms abolished neither the household registration system nor the conditions of entry for outsiders. Instead, they merely lowered the threshold for becoming a city resident. Moreover, Shijiazhuang's reforms proved to be only temporary: just two years after the scheme began, the local public security bureau raised the bar for residence, effectively preventing more migrant workers from joining the party.

Shijiazhuang's reforms are broadly representative of the national reform process, even a decade on. Few cities are keen to abandon *hukou* controls completely, because they fear that opening the floodgates will leave them bankrupt. To this day, local government officials cite the experience of Zhengzhou, the capital of Henan province, as evidence for retaining strict *hukou* controls. When Zhengzhou introduced similar reforms to Shijiazhuang in 2001, it was deluged with *hukou* applications, both from long-term migrants who had been living around the scruffy wholesale markets on the city's fringe and from residents of satellite towns hoping to boost their children's education prospects. Officials feared that an influx of newcomers would overtax infrastructure and services. In 2003, the city authorities admitted defeat and reimposed former restrictions on urban residency.

Other localities took a different approach. Over the past decade, fifteen provinces declared they would abolish the distinction between rural and urban *hukou* altogether, reclassifying every local resident under a new unified *hukou* scheme. A clutch of reports interpreted this reform as presaging a new age of equal rights for farmers and rural migrants. In reality, the reforms only applied *within* individual towns, cities or city districts, not across whole provinces. And most of the selected locales only contained a small proportion of local rural *hukou* holders, many of whom had long since stopped working on the land. Typically, farmers who lived on the city edge were granted urban *hukou* in exchange for giving up their land (although the benefits they received did not always match those enjoyed by urban natives).

Most importantly, the reforms only applied to farmers with a local *hukou*, not to the floating population of migrant workers. One of the provinces to introduce a new unified 'residents' category for all citizens was Guangdong – yet to this day both Shenzhen and Guangzhou maintain tough qualification criteria for outside migrants hoping to acquire a local *hukou*. Moreover, the shift in nomenclature has so far made little difference to many farmers. In Chengdu, which has slowly been dissolving the distinction between rural and urban *hukou* since the mid-2000s, few former rural *hukou* holders have gained urban social welfare. The distinction between rural and urban status remains in practice, if not in name.

By 2010, the urban *hukou* population had reached 460 million – meaning that well over 200 million people in China's cities were not entitled to receive most public services. Yet the reality is probably worse than the raw numbers suggest, as the urban *hukou* population figure is misleadingly high. It includes tens of millions of ex-rural *hukou* holders who only recently converted to urban *hukou*, and are not yet integrated into the social security system. And it almost certainly includes farmers reclassified as 'citizens' under unified registration schemes, most of whom receive few urban-style benefits. The gap between the urban haves and the 'rural' have-nots continues to widen.

城市化

Local *hukou* reforms have created a hotchpotch of policies in cities across the country. But one broad generalization can be made:

the liberalization of the old household registration system is more widespread in smaller cities than in big cities. All cities require outsiders to meet certain criteria to qualify for a local *hukou*, and the conversion criteria rise with the size of the city – a policy that is explicitly stated in China's 12th Five Year Plan. Big cities, which tend to have superior schools and health care, operate much more stringent policies than smaller cities. Applicants from non-local residents for big-city *hukou* are typically required to be extremely rich or highly educated. It is much easier to get an urban *hukou* in small urban centres, where social welfare and other amenities are inferior. But even there most new urban *hukou* are granted to local rural *hukou* holders, not to migrants from outside the local area.

Under the mishmash of rules implemented by local governments since the late 1990s, it is impossible for the vast majority of migrant workers to gain an urban *hukou*, especially as most congregate in large urban centres where the conversion criteria are especially high. Almost no migrant workers have a university degree, and only a tiny number of business-savvy outsiders have enough cash to buy their way in under the official channels. Beijing, for example, will only grant *hukou* to entrepreneurs who can invest a preposterous Rmb8 million (about US$1.25 million) to set up a company in the city. In some cases, the new barriers erected by local governments to permanent migration are harder to vault than the old ones.

It is not only migrant workers who suffer: transferring household registration between cities is difficult for urban *hukou* holders without money or connections. In Beijing, which probably maintains the most stringent *hukou* regimen in the country, even new graduates from the capital's universities struggle to gain a local *hukou*. Without a Ph.D. or Master's degree, the best option for lowly Bachelor's graduates is to find a local to marry. Even then, they must wait ten years before the authorities will believe their marriage is real – seven years longer than it takes for a foreigner married to a British citizen to gain UK citizenship. The situation is a little more optimistic for professional employees of big companies, which receive a yearly *hukou* quota from the Beijing public security bureau to help attract talented outsiders. Small private companies have much greater difficulty obtaining a *hukou* quota, although they can buy them from other companies whose quota remains unfilled. For desperate individuals, a thriving black market has emerged, with 'hukou vendors' claiming they can help new graduates purchase a Beijing residence permit for anywhere north of US$20,000.

The situation is much better for local rural *hukou* holders in the capital, who receive city residence when they graduate from university. All local rural residents in Beijing's fourteen satellite cities and thirty-three towns may apply for an urban *hukou* if they can prove a fixed urban residence and stable income for two years. But these *hukou* only entitle the holder to social services in the town in which they live, not in the city proper. The same policy applies to outsiders after five years, although few migrant workers can meet the residence and income conditions required.

Guangdong, by contrast, operates a points system to sort the skilled from the unskilled. Before applying for a *hukou*, long-term migrants must obtain a special, non-*hukou* residence permit and make social insurance contributions for several years. Applicants are then awarded points based on education, skills, social insurance contributions and voluntary work, and must gain a total of sixty points to qualify for a *hukou*. Most urban *hukou* are only available in smaller towns and cities, not in big urban centres like Guangzhou or Shenzhen. Again, few migrant workers are capable of meeting these conditions.

For most urban *hukou* holders, living without a local *hukou* is an inconvenience. They must pay extra for their children's schooling and for health care, and they may not be able to buy property or register a car without paying local taxes for several years. But it is rarely a reason to decline a better position away from their home town. As salaries have grown and the private sector has begun to provide the bulk of housing, local *hukou* have lost much of their lustre. Ambitious professionals have little choice but to pursue their careers in a handful of big cities, because that is where the good jobs are. Moreover, urban professionals always have the option of returning 'home' for medical treatment, or sending their children back for schooling.

The situation is much tougher for rural migrant workers, who are only half as likely as urban migrants to participate in local social insurance schemes through their employers. According to a 2009 survey by NBS, only 32 per cent of long-distance rural migrants had health insurance in their place of work, compared with 56 per cent of migrants with urban *hukou*. That proportion slipped to 24 per cent for pensions and 10 per cent for unemployment insurance. In a separate 2011 survey, the numbers were even worse: fewer than 20 per cent had either health insurance or a pension. Many rural migrant workers do not participate in any form of social security at all, and almost all remain outside the full employer-based urban social security net.

One problem is that the social security system is not designed for workers who frequently jump between jobs and cities. The system works fine for most urban residents, who usually have a fixed residence. But it is next to useless for migrants, whose temporary employment status prevents them from meeting the 'standard employment' criteria. Casual service workers, for example, rarely have the paperwork needed to join the social security system. Moreover, the difficulty of transferring social security accounts between localities means participation is impracticable for many migrant workers. To qualify for retirement benefit, workers must make fifteen years' worth of contributions to a single fund. They may cash their individual account if they move to another city, but in so doing they lose their claim to their employers' contribution, which is collected in a separate social pool. For this reason, the few migrant workers who do take out old-age insurance often end up subsidizing the pensions of urban natives.

The first step to solving these problems would be to create a more flexible social security system. Some experiments are being conducted. Zhejiang province, for example, allows migrants to make smaller social security contributions in return for more limited benefits – a sensible move given migrants' complaints about the high cost of participating in the standard urban social security scheme. And Shanghai has introduced a new comprehensive insurance system specifically designed for employees without a local *hukou*. But the key to creating a functioning national system is to make individual social security accounts truly portable, so that they can be conveniently moved between cities.

The administrative challenges of creating a genuinely national social security system are immense, but the social building blocks are increasingly in place. Migrant workers, although still highly mobile, lead more settled lives than they once did. In 2009, 57 per cent of migrants surveyed by NBS had worked in cities for more than five years, and 27 per cent for more than ten years. On average, migrants had been in the same job for four years. Moreover, the proportion of migrants bringing their family with them continues to climb, as a growing number of migrants see their future in the city. A large proportion of the second generation of migrant workers, those born in the 1980s and 1990s, have no intention of returning to the countryside.

As migrant workers settle in the city permanently, the case for extending social security to them will strengthen, while the administrative challenge of providing it will recede. Policy is already beginning to reflect this change. The Social Insurance Law enacted in July 2011 entitles migrant workers to transfer their pension, plus their medical and unemployment insurance, from one city to another. But it remains to be seen whether this will occur in practice.

城市化

Public support for *hukou* reform is strengthening. Liberal intellectuals, in particular, believe the current system is morally untenable. On 1 March 2010, on the eve of the annual meeting of China's parliament, thirteen newspapers in big cities across the nation made an unprecedented joint appeal to the government to speed up *hukou* reform. 'China has suffered under the *hukou* system for so long!' they declared in unison. 'We believe people are born to be free and should have the right to migrate freely, but citizens are burdened by outdated policies born in the era of the planned economy!' (Anderlini 2010; Jacobs 2010a; Branigan 2010). In near-identical front-page editorials, the newspapers urged the nation's parliamentary representatives to press for the dissolution of the 'invisible and heavy shackles of household registration'.

The rare coordinated critique of government policy came a few months after the Communist Party and the State Council declared further plans to relax *hukou* restrictions in small and medium-sized cities. Figuring the time was ripe to press their case, the editors of the Beijing-based *Economic Observer* persuaded their counterparts at other newspapers to come on board. Unfortunately, they misread the political winds. The Central Propaganda Department reacted incisively, instructing all the publications involved to remove the editorial from their websites. Zhang Hong, the deputy editor-in-chief of the *Economic Observer Online* and co-author of the editorial, was booted out of his job. And all talk of *hukou* reform disappeared from public debate overnight.

For more than a year, vested interests and conservative inertia seemed to have won the day. But liberal thinkers within the government system kept on making the case for reform. A consistent proponent was the Development Research Center (DRC), a think-tank directly under the State Council. In August 2011, the DRC published a book arguing that the government should create a fairer society in which migrant workers are able to enjoy the fruits of urbanization (DRC 2011). It bluntly stated that the failure to treat migrant workers as full urban citizens was responsible for much 'social disease and suffering'. Policy should focus, the book argued, on giving migrants full access to urban social services, including housing and welfare; integrating migrants into urban enterprises, with all the proper employment protections; and allowing migrant children to attend local schools free of charge.

Six months later, in early 2012, the State Council signalled that *hukou* reform was back on the political agenda. In a statement dated February 2011 but issued a year later, policymakers stated that long-term migrant workers and their families should be granted local *hukou* in prefecture-level cities. Provincial capitals and other big cities remain off limits, but the bar to enter urban society is gradually (glacially might be a better term) being lowered. They also instructed local governments not to tie all residents' eligibility for jobs, work training and schooling to their *hukou* status. Premier Wen Jiabao then told the annual meeting of the National People's Congress (NPC) that the government would 'give higher priority to registering rural migrant workers with stable jobs and permanent homes in cities or towns as permanent urban residents'.

This was hardly revolutionary stuff, and experience shows that all government talk about *hukou* reform deserves to be taken with a large pinch of salt. But a separate announcement by the Ministry of Public Security, which revealed that it would submit a plan for a new national residence system to the State Council within a year, suggests that real reform is once again being discussed in the highest echelons of government. The ministry said the draft proposal, which it was circulating around other government departments, would give migrants access to schools, health care, housing and social security in the cities in which they work. 'It will create conditions for the workers to enjoy equal basic public services and pave the way for their settling down in urban areas gradually,' MPS announced on its website.

Delinking access to basic services from *hukou* status has already begun in several localities nationwide. Since 2009, Shanghai, Shenzhen, Zhejiang, Guangdong, Jiangsu, Chongqing and Chengdu have introduced residence permit systems that entitle migrant workers to access local social services. Some permit systems – which operate independently of the national *hukou* system – offer easy access to an extremely limited number of services. Some, such as Shanghai's, set a high eligibility threshold but offer a comprehensive social insurance package. Other systems offer a mix of both, giving limited entitlements to temporary permit holders and full entitlements to permanent residents. MPS's announcement suggests these local residence permit schemes could be extended nationwide.

Interestingly, the ministry's plan is exactly in line with the recommendations made in a joint report published by the World Bank and the DRC in early 2012. *China 2030: Building a Modern, Harmonious, and Creative High-Income Society* argues that China should come up with a national framework to expand the coverage of registration permit systems among migrant workers, as an initial step towards providing social entitlements to migrant workers irrespective of their *hukou* status. At the same time, local governments should continue to lower the threshold for *hukou* conversion among local rural residents. '*Hukou* reform needs a phased strategy implemented over an extended period, with the end goal of *hukou* being a simple population registration system, delinked from social entitlements,' the report concludes (World Bank and DRC 2012: 366).

This 'phased expansion' of the residence permit system would begin by ensuring that all localities use similar criteria to determine who is eligible for a local permit. These would probably be based on years of local residence, stable accommodation, fixed employment and social insurance contributions, although the thresholds for each would continue to vary between localities. Once a national framework was in place, the system would gradually be rolled out across the country. The coverage of the system would gradually widen, beginning with all rural residents under the jurisdiction of the local prefecture-level city, then extending to all rural residents belonging to the local province, and ultimately opening up residence permits to rural migrants from beyond the province. 'Under such a common national framework, the residence permit could be rolled out nationally by the second half of this decade,' the report affirms (World Bank and DRC 2012: 367).

It is important not to exaggerate what an extension of local residence permits would mean for migrant workers. The benefits offered by existing residence permit schemes are far more limited than those enjoyed by local urban *hukou* holders. They only represent limited progress. But they do offer a potential path to *hukou* reform – a compromise between providing migrant workers with full urban benefits and giving them none at all. If MPS's plan becomes policy, it could mark a significant stage on the long road to more far-reaching *hukou* reforms. This will take time: even the World Bank's proposal does not envisage all residence permit holders enjoying the same social entitlements as local *hukou* holders until 2030.

The major stumbling block will almost certainly be cash. Who is going to pay for these expensive reforms? For thirty years, local governments have relied on cheap labour to attract investment and to build modern cities. The lack of legal protections afforded to migrant workers allows cities to maintain a large pool of casual workers at only a marginal cost. Under China's current fiscal system, local governments must bear the financial burden of allowing more migrant workers to receive benefits. For cash-strapped local governments, deliberately raising the cost of labour by extending more benefits to migrant workers makes little sense – especially when migrant wages are rising quickly of their own accord.

The solution is for the central government, which controls most taxes, to shoulder more of the financial burden of reform. Encouragingly, this message seems to be gaining some traction among policymakers. Du Ying, a deputy minister at the National Development Reform Commission, China's state planning body, has said that China should establish a cost-sharing mechanism to help pay for migrant workers' equal access to urban social benefits. Yet no substantial changes can occur without root-and-branch reform of China's fiscal system. This should be a priority for the new government under Premier Li Keqiang.

Reform of the current system is becoming more urgent: there is a strong political as well as a social case for extending urban welfare to migrant workers. Under the country's current social model, China risks breeding a huge and desperate underclass of economically

BOX 2.1 Down and out in Beijing

Cai Ansheng, a 65-year-old beggar living rough on the streets of Beijing, has little time for official proclamations about rural development. 'The Communist Party says fine things about how life in the countryside is improving, but it's all rubbish,' he says. 'People's lives in the village haven't changed much. When television reports show the premier visiting a village, they don't show what it's really like. What officials say is not ordinary lying – it goes way beyond that.'

Cai's anger is understandable. A double amputee, he spends his days flashing his shrivelled stumps to shoppers in Beijing's Sanlitun district, where diplomats rub shoulders with wealthy locals. Just a few steps away from Cai's position by the roadside, a Balenciaga store sells strappy shoes for US$1,000 a pair. As a rural resident without access to subsidized health care, Cai says he paid for his own amputation when his legs became diseased more than thirty years ago. Incapable of working his own land, he never found a wife and has no family to support him. He rents out his field in return for a subsistence income. 'That isn't enough to live on, even in the countryside,' he says.

Cai has been incontinent ever since he lost his legs. He stuffs a thick piece of material down his trousers to soak up fluids, but suffers from serious constipation. 'My shit is so dry that I have to pick it out by hand,' he says, waggling a brown gnarled finger. He sleeps rough under a canal bridge and has no means of washing. 'I came to Beijing two years ago because I couldn't live by myself at home without any help. Old people's homes are only for people with money. There was nothing else I could do.'

Cai gets around on a green, hand-propelled tricycle he bought in 1982. His possessions amount to a blanket, a pillow, an umbrella and an empty tea tin, plus the clothes he sits in – a black jacket and grey trousers cut off at the knee to reveal his missing legs. He says he plans to return home when the weather gets cold. 'I don't know if I'll come back to Beijing next year, because I could be dead by then,' he says. 'There's no point living like this. My life is just a waste.'

deprived residents with little civic responsibility. Ignored and often sneered at by native urbanites, rural migrants live and socialize together, excluded from urban society. For the most part, migrant workers still feel they can improve their lives; widespread discontent is surprisingly hard to find. But policymakers know that popular outrage could erupt if migrants ever felt the game was permanently stacked against them. As the number of disenfranchised migrant workers grows, reforming the *hukou* system will become a political necessity.

The Chongqing model: paying for the mayor's new clothes

Visitors to the Chongqing pavilion at the Shanghai Expo in the summer of 2010 were greeted by a huge map of the city-province that lit up to reveal a flaming phoenix. The rusting river port on the Yangtze, once a byword for corruption and gangsters, had been transformed into the fastest growing economy in the country. The symbolism was unmistakable: Chongqing had risen from the ashes.

At that time, the only surprise was that Chongqing chose a phoenix as its official emblem rather than a shining image of its charismatic Party secretary, Bo Xilai. In Bo's first two years in charge, Chongqing had smashed the mafia gangs that once ran the city-province, attracted billions of dollars of foreign investment, and begun to experiment with radical land and *hukou* reforms. It was an open secret that Bo, the son of a revolutionary hero, viewed success in Chongqing as his route onto the Politburo Standing Committee, the secretive cabal that runs Chinese politics. To shore up support from the left of the Party, Bo had resurrected revolutionary rhetoric and was encouraging Chongqing's pensioners to belt out the 'red' songs of their youth. His propagandists were even working on a book that described a distinctive 'Chongqing model' of development, a blueprint that could be copied by other provinces (see Su Wei et al. 2011).

Bo's star, of course, was extinguished in early 2012. After Chongqing's former police chief Wang Lijun dramatically fled to the US consulate in Chengdu, apparently in fear of his life, stories of his boss's corruption and brutality began to emerge. Bo was accused of turning Chongqing into his personal fiefdom, using his 'strike black' campaign against organized crime as a foil to crush political enemies. Tales of torture and mysterious deaths added to the intrigue. Leaders had watched in horror as Bo, a strutting peacock in a field of political uniformity, brazenly invoked Mao's memory to boost his own power base. Finally, they pulled rank. At his annual parliamentary press conference, Premier Wen Jiabao invoked 'the mistake of the Cultural Revolution' and rebuked Bo for his handling of the Wang Lijun case. Wen's public intervention was proof that Bo and his allies had lost the internal power struggle. The next day, Bo was summarily removed from his post and detained by state security – the most significant purging in the Communist Party's top ranks since the Tiananmen massacre in 1989.

Today, Chongqing's renaissance is indelibly associated with its disgraced former Party chief. With Bo's dismissal, the 'Chongqing model' has lost much of its lustre. Yet many of the economic and social reforms pursued over the past few years will continue. Under Bo's watch, Chongqing began to push through radical reforms to reshape the local economy, boost urbanization, and narrow the growing wealth gap between the city-province's urban and rural residents. Yet the real brain behind these reforms was Chongqing's technocratic mayor, Huang Qifan. Bo may have gone, but Huang – the power behind the throne – survives.

城市化

The social reforms being implemented to underpin economic growth in Chongqing are far more important than the faux-Maoist hoopla of the Bo years. Since 2007, when Chongqing and Chengdu were picked to pilot reforms to integrate urban and rural communities, Chongqing has begun to shake up entrenched national rules governing land, housing and the household registration system. Some of the reforms clearly give a big role to the state, and have been widely interpreted as 'leftist'. But other reforms are designed to increase the role of the market, especially in rural areas. Far from pandering to the leftist arm of the Party, policies to help free farmers from the land and give them greater individual property rights are all anathema to traditional Communist thinking.

Chongqing's urbanization goals are the country's most ambitious. Officials plan to move 10 million rural residents into cities from 2010 to 2020, pushing the urbanization ratio up from 50 per cent to 70 per cent. The reforms are designed to improve the living standards of rural people by reducing the massive labour surplus in rural Chongqing, where the average rural household farms less than one acre. Policymakers hope to raise rural incomes from a paltry 28 per cent of the urban average to a more respectable 40 per cent. The rural overcrowding in mountainous Chongqing is extreme, but the growing gap between rural and urban incomes is felt across the country. In 2000, the gap in average disposable income between urban and rural residents was Rmb4,000 (US$480); by 2010 that figure had more than trebled in local-currency terms to over Rmb13,000 (US$2,000).

Chongqing's policies to boost urbanization and reduce income gaps are essential ingredients in China's long-term effort to nurture domestic demand and rebalance the economy. If farmers move off the land for higher-paying jobs in the city, in theory they should turn into economically significant producers and consumers. The 12th Five Year Plan enshrines this policy, but does not say how quickly urbanization should be achieved. Localities are expected to come up with their own policies. Chongqing's approach is to persuade rural residents to give up their land rights and homesteads, and re-register as city residents. In exchange, they are supposed to receive housing and urban social services. The government has launched a huge public housing programme and claims it has found a sustainable means of financing the costs involved.

The first phase of Chongqing's rural-to-urban integration programme took place in 2010–11, when 3 million migrant workers with local rural *hukou* transferred to urban *hukou* (although it is unclear whether they were all immediately granted full urban benefits). These included roughly 2.3 million long-term migrant workers and their families with stable employment and accommodation in the city, and 700,000 university and high-school students. The second, trickier phase runs from 2012 to 2020. Officials hope to persuade 7 million resident farmers to swap their rural homesteads for a new life in the city – a very different proposition from giving urban *hukou* to migrant workers who are already settled. To smooth the transition, migrating farmers will retain their rural land rights for three years.

Mayor Huang Qifan likens *hukou* reform to a simple process of slipping off rough peasant garb for the more refined dress of the city. But persuading farmers to give up their land will be tougher than his metaphor suggests. Few migrant workers say they want a city *hukou*. 'I don't want to get rid of my rural *hukou*,' says Mr Li, a migrant worker taking a break in central Chongqing. 'Life is much better at home in the village, where I can grow my own food.' Li, whose village is a two-hour bus ride away, rents a cheap room with rickety wooden walls in Eighteen Steps. 'I come to the city to make money, that's all,' he says.

Mr Qin, a retired farmer from a village 200 kilometres away, lives in the city with his daughter, a 31-year-old accountant who owns her own apartment and has a city *hukou*. But Qin and his wife nominally retain their rural residency. 'By 2020, 20 million people in Chongqing will have urban *hukou*,' he says, knowledgeably. 'We could convert our rural *hukou* immediately, but we don't want to because we're old. What need do we have for a city *hukou*?' Many younger migrants feel the same way. Just 26 per cent of migrant workers interviewed in 106 cities by the National Population and Family Planning Commission in 2010 said they would choose to convert to an urban *hukou* if they had the choice.

The government's drive to promote urbanization risks pushing people into cities before they really want to move, or before jobs are ready for them. This problem is evident in Yuzui, a small town on the edge of a giant new economic zone that sprawls across the northern districts of Chongqing city. Farmers whose homes were bulldozed to make way for the zone now live in urban flats but survive on government handouts. Chen, a young farmer who runs errands on his motorbike for spare cash, says officials promised to pay US$10,000 for each acre of lost land and give relocated farmers an urban *hukou*. But several months after moving off his land, he had yet to receive any compensation. 'I preferred the farming life,' he says. 'Now I have to buy everything, but the cost of living in town is so much higher.' This is a common complaint from people used to living cheaply off the land.

A further problem is that the quantitative targets for urbanization give officials an incentive to trample on individual rights. In many cases, the conversion from rural to urban *hukou* is forced: university students with rural *hukou*, for example, cannot graduate until they register as urban residents. 'No one, including the government, is certain the urbanization target can be met,' says Zhou Wenxing, an associate professor of economics at Chongqing University. 'I'm worried they'll go too fast and won't make the reforms in a humane way.' In a review of Chongqing's urbanization policy, the World Bank warns that, while 'reform of the *hukou* system should be radical in its objectives, the pace at which such reform proceeds should be gradual… Launching a reform process without attention to potential risks is politically and socially dangerous' (World Bank 2009: 5, 13).

Lowering the barriers to social and economic integration is a laudable goal, but urbanization targets do not achieve this in themselves. If Chongqing's leaders fail to provide rural migrants with the social safety net they are promising, the city's urbanization policies could prove disastrous. The key to creating a sustainable urbanization process is, first, to promote continued jobs growth and, second, to remove barriers to people relocating to take those jobs. Moving fixed numbers of people regardless of whether they have employment in the city is an extremely risky policy. If the policy goes wrong, Chongqing's streets could end up teeming with a volatile mass of jobless, landless, impoverished farmers.

城市化

Policymakers in Chongqing believe the best way of alleviating fears about the urbanization process is to build more affordable housing for migrants. Most of the city's migrant workers currently live in private rented rooms like those in Eighteen Steps. In 2008–10, Chongqing officials say they tore down 12 million square metres of old housing and moved 450,000 people into bigger, better homes. Cui Zhiyuan, a former MIT professor who works as an adviser to the Chongqing government, says the driving force behind demolishing and rebuilding vast swathes of the city's slum housing was Bo Xilai. Bo initiated a similar scheme during his successful stint as mayor of Dalian, a port city in the northeast, in the 1990s. Chongqing's public housing scheme remains closely associated with Bo's personal brand of populist politics, but is also part of a much-publicized national plan to build 36 million units of subsidized housing by 2015. For this reason, Chongqing's housing reforms look safe.

New housing is sorely needed in Chongqing, not only to house the expected influx of new migrants but also to provide a better quality of life for the millions of migrant workers who already live there. City officials say they will complete 40 million square metres of subsidized public rental housing in 2010–12, by far China's most ambitious public housing programme. With units at 40–60 square metres in size, that should be enough to provide accommodation for around 800,000 households, or 2.4 million people. Half of the flats will be built in Chongqing city, and half in other urban areas within the larger city-province. Officials say rental units will be open to anyone who can prove a steady income and six months of social insurance payments, irrespective of whether they have a local *hukou*. Other cities maintain much stricter controls: Beijing's public rental units, for example, are only open to local low-income residents aged over 30. Huang Qifan says the long-term aim is to house 30–40 per cent of all urban residents in public rental units.

Sceptics doubt there is enough money in the city's coffers to pay for these costly plans. Chongqing University's Zhou Wenxing compares the government's tactics to those of the ruthless second-century warlord Cao Cao, who kept his starving men marching by promising a non-existent plum orchard around every corner. But supporters of the 'Chongqing model' thesis argue the city has developed a new mode of municipal financing that will keep it solvent. Cui, the former MIT professor, says the model is based on what he calls 'liberal socialism'. This basically means that profits from state-owned enterprises and sales of public land should subsidize low taxes and private business. From 2002 to 2009 the value of Chongqing's state assets rocketed from Rmb170 billion to more than Rmb1 trillion (about US$150 billion). Huang Qifan claims the huge increase in Chongqing's asset base allowed him to keep corporate tax rates at 15 per cent, make first-time mortgages tax-deductible, and push up education spending to 4 per cent of the city's GDP. The city government says that of the US$40 billion it spent in 2011, more than half went on projects to improve people's livelihoods.

Over the past decade, Chongqing's public finances were boosted enormously by rising land values. Planners acquired 200 square kilometres of land for urban development, often strategically located next to planned public infrastructure projects. They then injected much of this land into the city's eight local-government investment companies (LICs), which are responsible for building different types of infrastructure. In many cities, local governments acquire land for a public project, clear it for construction, and then sell it on to a real-estate developer for a profit. But Chongqing's LICs typically use their land banks as loan collateral to finance the construction themselves. When the project finishes, the surrounding land shoots up in value, and can be sold on at a much larger profit – often at ten times the pre-development price. One good example was the construction of the Chaotianmen Yangtze River Bridge in central

Chongqing, where the local government owned nearly 500 hectares of surrounding land. After construction, this prime real estate was sold on for a hefty profit. According to its supporters, this financial model created a virtuous cycle that allowed the city's LICs to keep borrowing against expected increases in land values.

Mayor Huang describes income from state assets as an extra financing 'pocket' supplementing taxation. Chongqing's smart new Grand Theatre, he boasts, was financed by state assets rather than by people's taxes. Huang also says he plans to use state-owned enterprise profits to subsidize the creation of 60,000 private 'micro-enterprises' to employ laid-off workers, graduates and new urban residents – including rural migrants. Huang says that up to 50 per cent of each company's start-up capital will be covered by the Chong-qing Finance Bureau and the local State-owned Assets Supervision and Administration Commission (SASAC), via dividends paid out by local state-owned enterprises. According to Cui, this 'indirect social dividend' was inspired by the Alaska Permanent Fund, which invests the US state's oil wealth and pays each resident an annual dividend.

If Huang succeeds in forcing state-owned enterprises to make a substantial contribution, it will constitute a noteworthy departure from central practice. Since the country's biggest state-owned en-terprises were restructured in the late 1990s and early 2000s, they have drawn huge benefits from the privileged position they occupy in the national economy, but have paid puny dividends. In 2010, total profits at the 122 central state-owned enterprises amounted to Rmb1.1 trillion (roughly US$170 billion). Only Rmb60 billion of this, a paltry 5 per cent, was returned to the central purse. There are plans to force these huge enterprises, which include all of China's oil majors, to pay more. But these powerful institutions, which operate as mini-fiefdoms within the Chinese state, will resist hard. By contrast, Chongqing's leaders claim that by financing infra-structure and subsidizing businesses with state assets, they are returning wealth to the people.

When all is said and done, however, Chongqing's financial arrangements do not look so unique. City officials remain reliant on land sales to fund many of their ambitious projects, a precarious financial model that depends on ever-rising land values. As the asset side of the city's balance sheet has ballooned, so too have its liabilities. Victor Shih, a former professor at Northwestern University in Illinois, reckons that Chongqing's total debts may exceed Rmb1 trillion – around US$160 billion. For example, the boom in public housing that is central to Chongqing's urbanization plan is being financed mostly by debt. Of the total building cost of Rmb100 billion (US$15 billion), the city government will provide about Rmb20 billion and the Ministry of Finance a further Rmb10–15 billion. The remaining 70 per cent will be financed by loans from commercial banks and China Development Bank, the nation's main policy lender. Most of the housing units will be built by Chongqing City Construction, a local-government investment company, which is waiving the 6–8 per cent return demanded by commercial developers.

Yet this pales into insignificance next to the cost of urbanizing 10 million rural migrants, with all the attendant social benefits. Chongqing estimates the initial cost of turning each migrant into a full city resident at Rmb67,000 (around US$10,000). City officials budgeted the cost of urbanizing the first batch of 3 million migrants in its grand plan at Rmb201 billion (US$30 billion): Rmb124 billion for urban social security costs and Rmb77 billion for land compensation costs. They say they expect employers and individuals to pick up most of the bill through dividends and social security payments, but it remains to be seen whether this is feasible. And even these costs will seem like small beer once the city government starts compensating the second batch of 7 million farmers that it plans to urbanize by 2020.

Worryingly, the Rmb67,000 cost of converting each migrant into an urban citizen does not even include long-term pension costs. Mi Hong, an economist at Zhejiang University in Hangzhou, reckons that Chongqing's pension fund will run short of money as early as

2018. By 2038, when many of today's migrants will be retiring, that gap will have grown to Rmb186 billion (US$28 billion). Another challenge will be building sufficient infrastructure to cope with the influx of new urbanites. Chongqing is planning to build 115 new schools, and the cost will be substantial. For the moment, the government is putting its faith in the urban land market, guessing that it can offset these costs by selling more lucrative urban construction land. But that is an extremely risky game to play.

城市化

Chongqing's ambitious *hukou* reforms put it ahead of many other cities, but its financial problems are representative of those nationwide. Perhaps the biggest problem under China's current fiscal system is that individual cities will be expected to pay for *hukou* reforms by themselves. At the national level, calculating the cost of providing for China's swelling urban masses relies on educated guesswork. Based on research in Jiaxing, Wuhan, Zhengzhou and Chongqing, the DRC estimates that providing lifelong social security for each new urbanite would cost around Rmb100,000 at 2010 prices (about US$15,000), of which Rmb80,000 will be provided by the public purse. If the central government dipped into its pocket, the reforms would become much more affordable.

Assuming that China extended urban benefits and welfare to 300 million migrant workers over the next twenty years, the DRC's calculations give a grand bill of Rmb1.5 trillion per year (US$230 billion), or 3.8 per cent of 2010 GDP. Stripping out Rmb20,000 per person, which the DRC assumes will be paid by individual and employer contributions, lowers the local government burden to Rmb1.2 trillion per year, or 3 per cent of GDP. To put that in context, total government expenditure was 22.6 per cent of GDP in 2010. The cost of meeting this extra burden, in other words, would require raising government spending to around 26 per cent of GDP – tough, but manageable. 'The cost to the public purse of urbanizing rural migrant workers is not unbearable,' the DRC concludes.

'The crux of the matter is whether governments have the ability to mobilize the funds' (DRC 2011: 43–4).

How hard finding the money proves to be will depend on a number of variables – not least the speed of urbanization and economic growth. But central policymakers need to make a decision about how urbanization and *hukou* reform will be funded. No one really knows the financial implications of pursuing a fairer, socially inclusive form of urbanization. When the central government finally decides it is time to end China's social apartheid and include rural migrants in the urban social welfare bill, it will need to contribute its fair share. Forcing local governments to bear the entire burden is unfeasible and potentially disastrous.

In the meantime, early evidence suggests that trouble is brewing in Chongqing, irrespective of recent political upheavals. Most rural residents do not want to give up their land, and officials have used coercion to meet their urbanization targets. Many rural migrants will not be able to afford public housing, and the local economy will struggle to create enough jobs for them. Chongqing's financial model rests on using state-controlled capitalism to realize broadly socialist ends. But there is a real possibility that Huang Qifan's financial wizardry may dissolve in a puff of smoke. The city's reliance on bank loans, obtained by deliberately jacking up land values, looks suspiciously similar to other dubious local-government financing models. If land values slide for any length of time, as they threatened to do in late 2011, Huang might appear less a true magician than a duplicitous conjurer.

How the fallout from the purging of Bo Xilai will affect Chongqing's long-term reforms remains to be seen. As the central government investigates companies and officials associated with Bo, reform could slow. Bo's fall may give ammunition to those critics who argue that Chongqing's land and *hukou* reforms are dangerous, and moving too fast – although many of these critics are on the left of the Party, with which Bo is now associated. But plans to boost urbanization were in train before Bo arrived in Chongqing in late 2007, and the city's development strategy has independent backing in Beijing. As a municipality under central government control and the focus of a long-term development plan in western China, Chongqing benefits from unusually strong government support. In May 2012, state media announced that China Development Bank would funnel extra funds into building low-cost housing and other infrastructure projects in the municipality. Chongqing's rapid development should survive the fall of its infamous ex-chief.

Chongqing is in the fortunate position of enjoying enormous state munificence. But the vast majority of localities in China enjoy nothing of the sort: they must fund urbanization reforms largely on their own. If China is serious about creating a fairer system of household registration, reform must be directed – and partly funded – from the centre. A Communist government is unlikely ever to abolish the *hukou* system completely because it is such a useful means of social control. But there is no reason, given time and political will, why China should not delink the allocation of social benefits from *hukou* status. Household registration could then become a simple social recording system, just as it is in Taiwan and Japan.

BOX 2.2 **City livin'**

Yu Changjiang dresses in the cotton shoes favoured by many rural folk, but his soft, pale skin marks him out as a city resident. Yu was born in 1969 in a village in east Sichuan, now part of Chongqing municipality. His journey from farm to flat shows how some rural migrants can successfully integrate into urban society.

Yu, whose name literally means 'Chongqing Yangtze River', has driven a yellow taxi in the city for five years. He talks with the sing-song, lisping accent of Chongqing, but also speaks passable Mandarin, unlike his family and friends back in the village, whose thick local dialect is impenetrable to outsiders. After twenty years in the city, he has developed a veneer of urban sophistication and is impressively knowledgeable about the world.

Yu's father died young, so he was brought up by his mother and uncle, living in a traditional rural homestead set around a dusty courtyard. As a boy, he walked to school through the village fields, which in springtime blazed with fragrant yellow rape flowers. After leaving school at 15, Yu began adult life as a farmer, spending two years knee-deep in the village paddy fields. But when he was 18, family contacts found him a job as a delivery boy 130 kilometres away in Chongqing city. As hundreds of millions of other rural migrants have done over the past thirty years, he moved to the city and found a bed in the company dormitory.

After five years of saving, Yu bought driving lessons. His family pooled their savings to buy a minivan for US$3,500, allowing him to make his own deliveries. By 2006, after working in the city for nearly twenty years, Yu bought his first apartment in Chongqing's Ban'an District for US$20,000, securing a 70 per cent mortgage from a local rural credit company, now part of the restructured Chongqing Rural Credit Commercial Bank. By 2011, the 90-square-metre apartment had trebled in value.

With his own city property, Yu decided it was time to convert from a rural to an urban *hukou*. Local residence regulations stipulated that he needed a university degree, but a friend introduced him to a government official, who helped him bypass the rules. Yu's wife, by contrast, maintains her official rural residence and, therefore, her right to farm a small parcel of land. 'My wife is still classified as rural,' he says, 'but we have both lived in the city for years and feel like urban residents.'

Yu and his wife intend to maintain their family's final link to the land, but they say life in the city is good. In 2007, Yu swapped his minivan for a taxi, boosting his monthly earnings to nearly US$500. He now has three years of urban pension payments under his belt and his daughter attends the local school for free. 'She is class monitor, and will have no problem getting into university,' he says proudly. 'Her grandfather is an uneducated farmer in the village, and cannot believe his granddaughter is receiving a good city schooling.'

BOX 2.3 **River town scrubs up**

One of the 'stars' in the Chongqing firmament is the grimy river town of Fuling, located on the confluence of the Yangtze and Wujiang rivers, 90 kilometres east of Chongqing city. Ringed by green mountains, Fuling remained economically cut off from the huge metropolis on its doorstep until an expressway opened in the late 1990s. Until then, a journey by river boat to Chongqing's passenger docks took the best part of a day; now the trip by car or rail takes little more than an hour. Much of the city still looks like the place of crumbling grey tenements and small family businesses described in Peter Hessler's lyrical 2001 memoir *River Town*. But Fuling today is expanding, and enjoying the first trickle of prosperity.

The district of Fuling district, which has a population of 1.2 million, is split almost equally between city residents and farmers. But the proportion of those people living in the urban area is projected to rise from around 650,000 today to 780,000 by 2020, pushing the district's urbanization rate up to 65 per cent. Local officials are trying to transform Fuling from a decrepit backwater into a smart satellite of Chongqing city. In 2009, they opened an impressive suspension bridge over the Wujiang, and they have built a new theatre and five-star hotel complex overlooking the city's two rivers. The hope is that rich tourists on river cruises to the scenic Three Gorges area will stop off on their way. Locals say that new streets and public areas, including a central square and riverside promenade, have made Fuling unrecognizable from the run-down city of a decade ago.

Yet more investment is needed to provide better housing both for local residents and for the steady inflow of migrants from the surrounding countryside. Dark, tumbledown houses by the river are slowly being demolished and replaced with new apartment blocks. Behind a new wall, built to protect the city from the rising water level caused by the Three Gorges Dam, luxury compounds are springing up on a former floodplain. These apartments sell for just one-third of their equivalent in Chongqing city, or barely one-tenth of the price of apartments 2,000 kilometres downstream in Shanghai. A spacious three-bedroom apartment with a river view can be had for just US$80,000. But they are unaffordable for most locals and represent an unattainable fairyland to migrant workers.

Take, for example, 40-year-old Zhen Zaoquan. Born in a poor village in rural Fuling, Zhen moved to the Pearl River Delta with his wife and young son in the 1990s, working for six years in a computer software factory in Guangzhou. In 2000, the family returned to Fuling, having scraped together enough cash to buy a cheap flat in the city. Under local household registration regulations, owning a property entitled the family to convert to an urban *hukou* – although Zhen first had to pay a fine to register his daughter, born in defiance of family planning regulations. Unable to find a good job in Fuling, Zhen sold his home to buy a car. He now taxis people and goods around the city, and rents a dingy old apartment for US$50 per month.

Zhen is one example of millions of Chongqing farmers who have been granted urban *hukou* over the past decade. Like most of them, he was barely compensated for his land and struggles to get by. To make matters worse, his shabby but cheap flat will soon be demolished. For Zhen and other migrants like him, access to subsidized public housing is vital to make urban life affordable. 'Where would someone like me find Rmb500,000 (US$80,000) for a new apartment?' he asks wistfully.

3

Farm versus Factory:
The Battle over Land

On 9 December 2011, a man from a fishing village in southern China died in police custody. The police blamed his death on a heart attack, but his corpse bore all the signs of a brutal beating, even torture. 'There were bruises all over, his hands were puffy, and there were bruises on his wrists,' the man's eldest daughter told a Hong Kong magazine. 'There were wounds and it looked like his thumbs had been pulled back and broken. On his back there were many marks showing he had been beaten or stamped on' (Reuters 2011).

Cruel deaths are not uncommon in China, but the killing of Xue Jinbo filled column inches across the world. Trouble had been brewing for months before Xue's death ignited open rebellion on the streets of Wukan, a village of 20,000 in the coastal province of Guangdong. Protests began in September after village cadres sold a pig farm owned by the village collective to a luxury housing developer. After more than a decade in which the village's farmland had been sold off to developers, plot by plot, the fragile peace in Wukan shattered. Farmers ransacked government buildings and destroyed police cars, waving placards demanding their land back. The authorities responded by sending in police and plain-clothed thugs to beat the protestors, before eventually agreeing to allow villagers to choose representatives to negotiate with them for a settlement. One of those men was a middle-aged butcher, Xue Jinbo.

So far, so normal: local protests over illegal land seizures and inadequate compensation occur every day in dozens of villages across China. When such protests occur, the authorities strike hard but are sometimes forced to compromise with irate farmers. But in early December, when security agents abducted Xue and four other village representatives, war erupted in Wukan. When the news of Xue's death emerged, villagers chased all officials and police out of Wukan, blockaded the village, and armed themselves with steel-tipped bamboo spears, hoes and pitchforks. In what some reporters dubbed the 'Siege of Wukan', the local government surrounded the village with 1,000 paramilitary police and prevented all food and goods from getting in. The stand-off lasted ten days until, finally, senior provincial officials stepped in, promising to halt land sales, hold village elections, redistribute stolen land and crack down on corrupt officials.

Reporters and analysts have picked over the causes and significance of the Wukan protests. Many have focused on the number and virulence of 'mass incidents' – an ill-defined term used to describe all sorts of social unrest, from drunken brawls in the street to citywide protests. One expert on civil unrest, Sun Liping of Tsinghua University, estimates there were over 180,000 'mass incidents' in 2010, although the Chinese government has not released data on civil unrest for years. What is truly significant about the Wukan protests is that they were not that unusual. They were larger and more protracted than most; but villagers protest against land disputes, often violently, all over the country every day. Excitable reports that violent uprisings of this sort could spell the end of Communist rule are nonsense: China is a very big place, the Communist Party remains very powerful, and local protests have little impact on the national balance of power. Far more interesting is what Wukan says about the nature of urbanization in China and the failure of collective land ownership to protect farmers' land rights, and how this fits into the nationwide debate about land reform.

Currently, land in China is divided into two types: urban and rural. Urban land is owned by the state but leased for seventy-year periods to developers, companies and homeowners. Rural land belongs to the collective, which leases parcels of land to farmers for extendable thirty-year periods. Rural land is further divided into two broad types: farmland and rural construction land, occupied by homesteads, public buildings and roads. The collective has the right to sell the land it owns, but cannot sell it directly for urban development. Only local governments have the legal power to turn collectively owned land into state-owned urban land, which can then be used for construction. Because urban construction land is worth far more than rural land, local governments are able to pocket the difference between the low price they pay for rural land and the much higher price they can sell it for as urban construction land. This lucrative game is a huge money-spinner for local governments, which rely on land sales for a substantial chunk of their income.

Collective ownership of land is supposed to protect farmers from rapacious landlords and developers. But all too often it merely makes them the victims of greedy village chiefs and local officials, who sell communal land to developers for enormous personal profit. If the developers have good connections with the local government, they should have little problem converting their new parcel of farmland into state-owned land for urban construction. In Wukan, villagers blamed the village head for selling off hundreds of hectares of collectively owned land over many years. As long as power is effectively concentrated in the hands of a few unaccountable village representatives, land abuses will continue to occur.

One step towards solving the problem of illegal land grabs is to follow Wukan's lead and allow villagers to elect their own ruling committees in fair elections. Under the rigorous system put in place in Wukan, villagers elected an eleven-man committee to supervise a second election of thirteen village representatives. These representatives now monitor the governance of the village committee, which was elected in a third, separate, vote. This convoluted system will make it far more difficult to concentrate power in a few hands – but it is no guarantee. A much surer way of protecting individual farmers' rights would be to abolish collective ownership and introduce clear, individual property rights. Since there will always be demand for land, China must find a fair and practicable way of ensuring that farmers are properly compensated when their land is sold.

As China embarks on ambitious *hukou* reforms and more farmers leave their land for the city, policymakers must address the issue of private land rights. China's Property Law affirms that state and collective land are entitled to the same level of protection, yet rural households still face the risk of expropriation. Individual property rights are not only needed to protect farmers from greedy officials; they are a necessary step towards creating a healthier form of ur-banization, grounded in the principle of allowing farmers to gain more value from their land. If China is serious about improving the lives of its rural populace, simply investing in the countryside and allowing people to change their residence status is not enough: individual farmers must be given effective ownership of their land.

城市化

The story of Chinese land reform begins after the Communist triumph in China's civil war in 1949, when Mao Zedong and his comrades set about creating a Communist utopia fuelled by the collective muscle of the nation's farmers. Land was expropriated from landlords, redistributed and divided up between collective farms. In the late 1950s and early 1960s, as China pursued a series of disastrous economic policies, the collective farms helped to spread mass starvation in the countryside. During the Great Leap Forward in 1958–61, when farming collectives dropped their hoes in favour of smelting pig iron in backyard steel furnaces, it is estimated that anywhere between 18 million and 45 million people died. Collective farming was not responsible for this crazy policy, but it made the effects far worse. Individual farmers had no incentive to produce more than the quotas required, and leaders of village collectives lied about imaginary bumper harvests that were never collected from the fields.

In 1978, at a meeting known as the Third Plenum of the 11th Central Committee, China's new paramount chief Deng Xiaoping and senior Communist leaders finally abandoned the disastrous experiment with collective farms. Over the next five years, the collectives were replaced by over 200 million family farms, operating under the new 'household responsibility system'. The former collective, typically composed of all the members of a village, retained ownership of the land. But households were given the right to farm individual plots, allowed to grow what they wanted, and told they could sell anything they produced in excess of state quotas. The results were spectacular: in the decade or so following these reforms, agricultural output doubled and household incomes trebled. Boosted by the growth of township and village enterprises, the rural economy surged.

In the 1990s, however, the pendulum swung back to the cities. Over the past twenty years, urban incomes have grown more quickly than rural incomes, and the gap between the living standards in China's villages and cities has widened to a chasm. Critics of the household responsibility system pin much of the blame on farmers' lack of property rights. Rural villagers have no right to sell their homestead or mortgage the farmland assigned to them. By contrast, urban residents enjoy the right to sell and mortgage their homes (even if the land on which they are built remains state owned). Since the early 2000s, when the fledgling urban property market took off and housing prices soared, many millions of urban residents have flipped their way up the housing ladder and become rich. But farmers remain locked out of the property market and unable to capture most of the latent value of their land.

Policymakers have long recognized this problem, but root-and-branch land reform is ideologically unpalatable. Along with state ownership of the country's biggest enterprises, collective ownership of land is one of the only old Communist policies that remain sacrosanct. Advocates of land reform point at how China's cities have been transformed since the urban housing stock was privatized in the late 1990s – itself a major blow to Communist orthodoxy. They argue that enhancing farmers' land-use rights will help to redistribute land more efficiently, raise rural incomes, produce a more sustainable pattern of urbanization and, ultimately, help to stimulate domestic demand. But Communist hardliners and some well-meaning conservatives worry that liberalizing the land tenure system risks returning farmers to the dark old days of feudal China when, according to Party propaganda, peasants were rent slaves bound to rapacious landlords. Giving uneducated farmers the right to transfer their land, they fear, will allow a new class of unscrupulous land barons to monopolize the country's farms. Far from creating a mass of consumers, too much reform risks breeding a lumpenproletariat of landless peasants crammed into urban slums.

Against this backdrop, the central government has spent twenty years slowly piecing together a legal framework for stronger rural property rights. The rule of thumb has been to give farmers more rights to their land while studiously avoiding any hint of privatization. The first important step came in 1998, when revisions to the Land Management Law extended land-use rights from fifteen to thirty years and required villages to issue written land-use contracts to every farm household. Then, in 2003, the Rural Land Contracting Law prohibited village collectives from 'readjusting' land to account for the changing size of households during the thirty-year contract term. In principle, the move created secure and marketable land-use rights, allowing farmers to lease or trade their plots, although not to sell them.

Proponents of land reforms argue that creating a land market will unlock the monetary value of China's 120 million hectares of farmland. They echo the thinking of Peruvian economist Hernando de Soto in his influential book *The Mystery of Capital*, in which he argues that clear property rights can realize the 'dormant' value in land (de Soto 2000). This 'dead capital', de Soto maintains, merely needs to be 'brought to life' via clear property rights allied to markets. Evidence from other East Asian countries, notably South Korea and Taiwan, supports his case. In the 1950s, Taiwan's land tenure reforms provided tenant farmers with full private ownership of their land, setting the platform for the island's economic miracle. In the decade following the reforms, annual rice yields grew by 60 per cent and farm incomes leaped by 150 per cent. Higher incomes translated into much higher consumption of clothing, housing and household objects.

China has no formal plans to follow Taiwan's lead and privatize rural land ownership. Indeed, China's nominally Communist leaders studiously avoid any mention of private ownership. But a motley bunch of land reforms are gathering momentum, even if overall progress remains sluggish. Some of the reforms are sanctioned by the central government; others are promoted at the local level. And some, controversially, even have a whiff of privatization about them.

The first sign that Beijing was genuinely serious about promoting land reform came in 2008, when Communist leaders in the Third Plenary Session of the 17th Central Committee passed a fusty-sounding document named the 'Resolution on Some Major Issues in Rural Reform and Development'. The Resolution states that farmers may subcontract, lease, exchange or swap their land-use rights, and promises to extend farmers' thirty-year land-use rights indefinitely. The Resolution came exactly thirty years after the 11th Central Committee enacted the previous land reform plan, which marked the start of Reform and Opening. The date was hugely significant. Cheng Li, an expert on China's high politics at the Brookings Institution, predicts that future historians will come to regard 2008's Resolution as 'a landmark event in contemporary China' (Li 2009: 1).

Li summarizes the principal objectives of Hu Jintao's land reform plan as 'three moves': first, allowing land-use rights to move from one farmer to another (normally via simple land transfers); second, helping surplus rural labourers to move to cities and become urban residents; and, third, encouraging financial loans and investment to move into rural areas. Chen Xiwen, the director of the Office of the Central Leading Group on Rural Work, said the new policies were designed not only to strengthen the legal framework for land transfers but also to protect farmers from land grabs by local governments – by far the greatest source of unrest in rural China.

The reforms solidify farmers' property rights, giving them greater confidence to rent out their land or invest in new crops or technologies. Raising incomes for the hundreds of millions of farmers who wish to stay on the land is a necessary counterpart to China's aggressive urbanization policies. Unless agricultural productivity continues to rise as urbanization proceeds, the supply of farm produce will not keep up with demand, and inflation will wipe out the gains from higher incomes. For those farmers who do wish to migrate to the cities, the ability to rent out their land gives them an additional stream of income to help pay their bills in the city. Stronger rural property rights are therefore a step towards creating a healthier form of urbanization.

Two cities were prepared to launch land reforms from the go: Chengdu and Chongqing. In 2007, southwest China's largest cities were chosen to pilot land reforms designed to integrate rural residents into urban communities and narrow the wealth gap between urban and rural areas. Their first solution was to use property exchanges to open up agricultural land transfers to market forces. Land transfers are increasingly common across the country, but contracts are often drawn up on a casual, verbal basis. The introduction of an exchange offers a way to regulate and boost the scale of land transfers. Their second – and most innovative – solution was to extend the system to allow farmers to sell their rural construction land-use rights to urban developers. The day after the Third Plenum finished, Chengdu opened a rural property exchange. One month later, Chongqing announced that it would establish its own rural land exchange.

Both exchanges are designed to increase farmers' incomes and facilitate rural-to-urban migration. They allow farmers to transfer assets and land-use rights to other farmers or agribusinesses in exchange for lump-sum payments or annual rent. And, crucially, they allow farmers to receive cash or a new home, sometimes in the city, in return for selling the right to their rural construction land. The exchanges enable farmers to find buyers and fix prices, allowing them to leave their land with money in their pocket. Reforms in both cities officially remain at the experimental stage, but the domestic media have reported that policymakers are considering adopting similar land exchanges nationwide. If they do, Chengdu and Chongqing will become templates for national reforms that could revolutionize the rural economy and massively boost rural-to-urban migration.

BOX 3.1 Flogging the fields

China's leaders often say that improving the lives of China's more than 600 million farmers is one of their top priorities. Their policy has focused on abolishing rural taxes, improving rural infrastructure, and subsidizing purchases of household goods. But a 2011 survey by Landesa, a US-based non-profit organization, suggests progress has also been made on another crucial issue: developing a market in farmland.

One notable consequence of this is a recent influx of investment by larger-scale agribusiness. There are also undesirable side effects: more farmers are getting kicked off their land by unscrupulous local authorities. But if these abuses can be curbed, the trend promises to help boost farm productivity and support the urbanization drive that China's leaders want to power future growth. Thirty years after China gave households responsibility for their land, the transition to corporate farming has finally begun.

Since 1998, China's farmers have been given thirty-year, extendable rights to farm specific pieces of land. Local governments are obliged to provide each household with a certificate outlining what land is theirs to farm, plus a contract giving them legal ownership over the land rights. By solidifying these rights to land, so the thinking goes, farmers are better able to realize the value of their chief asset. Stronger property rights give farmers an incentive to invest in their land, which boosts their productivity and thus their income. And if farmers see better opportunities elsewhere, they can work for a wage and earn additional income by leasing their land-use rights to other farmers.

The Landesa survey, the fifth in a series done in cooperation with Beijing's Renmin University and Michigan State University, shows that improved documentation of farmers' land-use rights is indeed boosting agricultural productivity. The report, which covered 1,564 households in seventeen provinces in 2010, found that 63 per cent of farming families had been issued with land-use rights certificates and 53 per cent with land-use rights contracts.

Farmers receiving such documents were nearly twice as likely to make long-term investments such as building greenhouses or planting orchards. Four in every five farmers who made new investments did so within a year of receiving their certificate or contract, and these investments boosted each household's net annual income by almost US$2,500, equivalent to the average rural household income in 2009. Landesa estimates the gross income from those investments at Rmb454 billion nationwide (US$67 billion), nearly four times the Rmb123 billion spent on rural subsidies that year. Still, there are many farm households who have yet to benefit: only 44 per cent had been issued both land-use rights documents, and nearly three out of ten had no document at all.

Transactions enabled by these land-rights documents have picked up since a 2008 decision by China's central leadership to encourage transfers of rural land. About one in eight farmers had participated in a market transfer over the past three years – usually a type of lease, since the outright buying and selling of farmland is banned. While still relatively small, the rural land market can be rewarding. Landesa estimates that the median annual rent of farmland rose to US$660 per hectare in 2010 from US$560 in 2008.

Demand for farmland now increasingly comes from agribusinesses and real-estate developers, which accounted for nearly 40 per cent of land rentals in 2010, up from 30 per cent in 2008. A quarter of the villages surveyed had leased large tracts of land to companies or big individual investors, with each corporate holding averaging 37 hectares, equal to nearly one hundred times the average household landholding in those villages. Greater consolidation of farmland and more intensive farming – two aims of the 12th Five Year Plan – are vital steps towards creating a modernized, efficient farming sector.

Yet, unsurprisingly, abuses are common: nearly half of the leases to corporations came following pressure from local governments, which simply instructed farmers to lease the land in 16 per cent of cases. One quarter of these arrangements illegally exceed farmers' thirty-year tenure, and a third illegally use at least some of the leased land for non-agricultural purposes, such as building factories. The incentive for cash-strapped rural county governments to use farmland to attract corporations is strong.

The growth of the rental market also coincided with an upswing in land requisitions. Nearly 40 per cent of the villages surveyed had experienced at least one land taking since thirty-year rights were introduced in 1998, and land was requisitioned in more than one in ten villages in 2010. This may be related to the huge increase in land supplied for urban housing, which the central government ordered as part of its drive to cool down property prices.

Landesa's findings jibe with a report by the China Construction Management and Property Law Research Centre in Beijing, which found that 2010 was the worst year on record for forced housing demolitions. More farmers than ever are being forced off their land and out of their homes. Landesa concludes that the 'growing pattern of acquisitions of farmers' land rights ... threatens to gravely undermine farmers' tenure security and all the benefits which such security brings' (Landesa 2011). It recommends reforming the Land Management Law to improve the due process of rural land takings procedures, following the example of the much stricter provisions made in the law on urban land takings. And it suggests restricting corporate farming by limiting agribusinesses' agricultural land holdings and requiring informed consent from affected farmers.

Yet greater consolidation of farmland and more investment by agribusinesses are not necessarily a bad thing. The key is that farmers freely transfer their land rights, rather than get pushed off their land by rapacious officials and corporations. This will be extremely tough for China to achieve, given the incentives local officials have to abuse the system. But China's rural population is so large, and average farming plots so small, that urbanization and some consolidation of farm land are necessary. The average rural household today farms less than half a hectare of land. This is enough to produce only a subsistence-level income, which is why so many rural people have to work off the farm as well.

China's economic growth over the past twenty years has relied in large part on moving farmers from unproductive farming jobs into more productive jobs in cities. According to the government's own reasonably conservative projections, China can expect to move around 250 million people into cities by 2030, taking its urbanization rate past 65 per cent. This would nearly halve the current number of 200 million rural households, leaving each farming family with around 1 hectare of land – precisely the size of farm that Landesa argues supported the economic take-off of Japan, South Korea and Taiwan.

Improving the lives of China's farmers, and narrowing the income gap between the countryside and the cities, will require greater respect for rural land rights. But it will also require more farmers to trade these rights for a new life in the city.

Yours to sell: the great land-credit experiment

Chengdu, the capital of Sichuan province, is known for its teahouses and laid-back pace of life. During the Tang dynasty it was home to the great classical poets Li Bai and Du Fu, and remains today the most important centre of learning in west China. But Chengdu is also one of the fastest-growing urban areas in the country, with a population of 7 million packed into the city proper and a further 7 million living in smaller satellite towns and the surrounding country-side. Chengdu is frantically battling to keep up with its rougher local rival Chongqing, which the central government has crowned the 'dragon head' of development in China's relatively poor western provinces.

For cities across China, urbanization is a doubled-edged sword: boosting the number of urban residents is good for economic and social development, but the cost of providing migrants with social insurance is potentially crippling. Chengdu intends to turn 1 million of its rural residents into urban citizens by 2017, and must somehow find a way to pay for this. The city has a registered local population of around 12 million, plus a floating population of 2 million migrant workers. Of the registered population, 5 million are classed as rural.

To meet its urbanization target, the city government is trying to persuade farmers to leave their ultimate source of financial security: their land. Between 2008 and 2011, Chengdu registered all rural property in the municipality, the first step to establishing clear and tradable property rights. Government officials were charged with consolidating tiny individual patches of land into larger household plots and arbitrating household land disputes – a stressful process that caused scores to quit. The aim of the registration process was to clarify land-use rights by providing every household with a single contract; consolidating household plots was designed to prepare the way for industrialized farming. Even after this arduous process, there are still many more plots than contracts.

Urban construction land is a precious commodity in China. In 2006, the central government announced that China would maintain a minimum 120 million hectares of agricultural land – known as the 'red line' – to ensure that the country could feed itself. Since current national farmland is already very close to this minimum level, city governments face the conundrum of how to increase the supply of urban land while protecting farmland. Their solution is ingenious: create 'new' land. The process involves turning rural construction land into farmland, thereby creating a net gain in farmland. Each unit of reclaimed farmland creates one unit of construction land quota that can be used elsewhere, normally on the city edge where demand for land is greatest.

Land swaps are common across China, but only Chengdu and Chongqing have a system of creating land credits, effectively derivatives, to sell on an exchange. In theory, this should match more buyers to sellers, and make it far easier for farmers in remote villages to swap their homesteads for urban housing. The process involves finding a collective of farmers who agree to vacate their homesteads and move into new housing that takes up less space. If a whole village can be persuaded to abandon their homesteads, the farmers may be housed in new urban apartments on the edge of the old village or in the nearest town or city. When farmers' homes are demolished, the construction land on which they stood is recultivated and returned to agricultural use. Government agencies inspect the land and issue a credit, known in Chongqing as a *dipiao*, for the amount of new agricultural land created. The land credit is then auctioned on the city's rural property exchange. Real-estate developers who wish to build on a greenfield site approved for urban construction must first purchase a land credit for the equivalent amount of farmland. The buyer gains the right to develop a similar amount of agricultural land on the outskirts of the city, which it must purchase as usual from the local government.

One way of thinking of the system is that it creates a new property right – the right to develop rural construction land – and enables individual farmers to profit from the sale of this right. And because land swaps effectively allow a farmer to sell the right to develop land elsewhere, rather than to develop his specific plot, the system also has a redistributive function. In effect, a portion of the premium paid by property developers to convert rural land to urban use is returned to farmers living far from the city. In this way, even farmers who do not wish to migrate to the cities can cash in on China's urbanization bonanza.

Land trading in Chengdu began with the reconstruction effort following the devastating Sichuan earthquake of May 2008, which destroyed millions of homes north of the city. The city government allowed farmers who lost their homes to swap land across four city districts and one county. The land where their former homesteads stood was cleared and turned into farmland, and the farmers moved into urban homes, retaining the right to farm or trade their old agricultural land. When the policy proved a success, it was extended to all rural residents as part of Chengdu's urbanization push. At this point, no land credits were involved and the price of new urban construction land was set by the authorities. But in late 2008, Chongqing picked up the baton and began trading *dipiao* on its rural land exchange. Inspired by its neighbour, Chengdu launched its own scheme in 2010.

The city governments in Chengdu and Chongqing promote land credits as a novel way to raise rural incomes. But their prime motivation for launching the scheme was to boost their own land sales and fill government coffers. For government officials, the brilliance of the system is that it speeds up the process of urbanization while simultaneously creating funds to finance it. Indeed, the early success of Chengdu's first auction of land credits seemed to embolden the city government to press ahead with expensive new *hukou* reforms. Regulations issued at the end of 2010 stated that all Chengdu citizens – including 5 million farmers – could freely move into the city and register as urban citizens. The government says these new urbanites will receive full urban benefits, including education and health care, without having to give up their rural property in exchange. It also says it will build enough housing in 2011–15 to accommodate 1 million new urban residents. If the Chengdu government is as good as its word, this would represent a huge breakthrough for *hukou* reform.

As ever, the key constraint is financial. Chengdu's policymakers reportedly carried out a comprehensive risk assessment of the proposed reforms in 2010, which concluded that the city could afford to expand urban-style social security into rural areas and manage larger inflows of farmers. This calculation appears to have been based on an assumption that land sales, boosted by land-credit trading, would continue to raise sufficient revenue streams to pay for a faster pace of urbanization. Yet just two weeks after Chengdu's new *hukou* regulations were issued, the Chengdu rural property exchange suddenly announced that the second round of land credit auctions would be suspended. Suddenly, an expected revenue stream dried up.

No explanation was given for the suspension, but the decision was probably taken centrally. The national authorities have consistently expressed their concern that land swaps are being abused. Corrupt local officials and village cadres have every incentive to persuade, or force, villagers to vacate their homes. These farmers may end up with inadequate compensation or marooned in modern apartments far from their fields, with nowhere to raise their hens and pigs. One explanation is that leading rural affairs official Chen Xiwen, a strong critic of unsanctioned land swaps, intervened to protect farmers from being pushed off their land. Another is that provincial leaders feared that land credits were being sold with no reclaimed farmland to back them up. Whatever the reason, the suspension of land auctions blew a hole in Chengdu's financial projections, leaving the city's ambitious officials fearful that their expensive *hukou* reforms would be squashed before they had even begun.

In the event, a notice posted on the rural property exchange four months after the closure, in April 2011, announced that the land-credit auctions would resume. It contained a long list of conditions and legal requirements, emphasizing that farmers must only leave their land voluntarily, and that any net gain in land belonged to the collective. It also stated that that land inspections by several departments were required before land credits could be issued. Whether all of these regulations are adhered to, in a country where laws are routinely ignored, is a different matter.

城市化

Chongqing's experience of *dipiao* trading is more positive than Chengdu's, where land credits still play only a small role in the city's land market. In late 2011, after three years of trading, Chongqing's leaders proclaimed their system a spectacular success. They said *dipiao* trading had allowed thousands of farmers to pocket significant sums of cash, aided urbanization, improved rural living conditions, and provided much-needed land for urban development.

The government used a report on state-run Chongqing Television to make its case. It focused on villagers in Pengshui county, a backward and rugged area just over the border from Guizhou, China's poorest province. Many traditional homesteads here are empty because their owners have left to work in the city. Made of wood and tamped earth, the empty houses nestle among steep, water-filled rice terraces that glisten in the subtropical sun. More than 3 million hectares of land sit under unused homesteads, according to an estimate by the Chinese Academy of Social Sciences. In Chongqing, more than 50,000 hectares are wasted in this way, over 2 per cent of the municipality's total farmland. Since Chongqing is only about 25,000 hectares above its agricultural 'red line', recultivating this land makes clear sense.

According to the report, the *dipiao* system enabled villagers in Pengshui to demolish unused homesteads, recultivate the land, and sell the net gain on to developers far away in the city. Young villagers working in the city used their compensation money to open businesses, suggesting that the *dipiao* system is a viable way of promoting urbanization. Grinning farmers who chose to demolish their rambling homesteads and move into consolidated modern housing on the edge of the village claimed they could not believe how much money they had made. One apparently overjoyed farmer showed reporters the 4,000 chicks he had bought with some of his compensation. His new house, a concrete box tiled with fake brick, was far less picturesque than his old one. To a sentimental Western eye, this might seem a raw deal – but the farmer appeared delighted with this more modern accommodation.

Government officials say the *dipiao* system brings a number of benefits. First, it boosts farmers' property-based income. An average

Chinese farmer makes just Rmb5,400 a year (about US$850), of which just 3 per cent comes from assets. Selling *dipiao* is an innovative way to increase farmers' income from their chief, and in most cases only, asset – their land. Farmers are entitled to receive a minimum of Rmb1.4 million (US$225,000) per hectare, more than they would expect from an ordinary land transfer. In practice, they often receive a considerably higher rate of compensation (although, because the average rural household in Chongqing farms just one-third of a hectare, the sum received per household will be smaller). In addition, those farmers who choose to continue farming gain the reclaimed land under their homestead, typically enough to bring in an extra US$150 per year. They also get paid for clearing the construction land and turning it into fields, and they can sell any useful building materials taken from the dismantled house.

Second, officials say the *dipiao* system is prising open rural financial reform. Since 2011, Chongqing has allowed the certified land created by land swaps to be used as collateral for securing a mortgage – finally enabling farmers to realize some of the value of their 'dead capital'. According to official data, farmers borrowed Rmb15 billion (about US$2.5 billion) in the first year of the scheme. Chongqing set up a special risk fund to reassure banks that feared that any loans made to farmers would go bad, and agreed compensation would run to 30 per cent of losses. Allowing farmers to mortgage their agricultural land-use rights is an enormous step towards the privatization of land.

Third, officials say that *dipiao* are a useful extra source for improving rural conditions under a scheme officially dubbed 'building the new socialist countryside'. They view it as an indispensable means of helping to shrink the development gap between the city and the villages. Individual households are supposed to receive 85 per cent of income from *dipiao* sales, while the remaining 15 per cent goes to the village collective to improve village infrastructure and pay for social welfare. Selling *dipiao* further helps to raise incomes by allowing farmers to cash in their land and move to the city. For this reason, officials contend, the *dipiao* system can help boost rural welfare while simultaneously creating a more sustainable model of urbanization.

The government claims *dipiao* trading has been an unqualified success. The average compensation for farmers who give up their land in return for an urban *hukou* is around Rmb80,000 (US$13,000), but farmers who trade their land under their homesteads via the *dipiao* market receive considerably more, thanks to the much higher value of urban construction land. According to government figures for the first three years of *dipiao* trading, 6,000 hectares of land were sold, more than 9,000 hectares of rural construction land were cultivated as farmland, and farmers received Rmb17.5 billion (nearly US$3 billion). By the end of 2011, *dipiao* were used in two out of every three land purchases – a truly impressive achievement, if the figures are accurate. Chongqing's cheerleaders claim the *dipiao* system offers a new model of land management that can transform rural finance, and argue that it should be rolled out nationwide. The positive spin is designed to challenge critics on the Party's left, who fear that unscrupulous officials and developers will rob farmers of their land and leave unemployed migrant workers with nowhere to live.

One of the fiercest critics of Chongqing's reforms is Hu Jing, a professor at South China Normal University in Guangzhou, who condemns 'armchair theorists and government officials' for risking farmers' welfare. 'Contracted land is a special form of security. It is a substitute for unemployment benefits and old-age pensions,' he declared in a fiery attack in the *China Left Review*. 'The household responsibility system is the legacy of the millions of peasants who sacrificed their blood and lives to find the right path to gain land rights in the past century… [What] is the Chongqing government thinking by moving to "actively promote the transfer of land" at a time when it hasn't even provided peasants with an alternative social safety net?' (Hu Jing 2008).

An investigation by the *China Economic Times* suggests that Professor Hu was right to be concerned. In May 2010, the newspaper reported on the situation in Kongmu village in Chongqing's Jiangjin district, where thirty-two households were among the first batch of farmers to trade their land via *dipiao*. Local officials claimed that households volunteered to have their homes demolished, and that all the proper procedures were followed, including compensating the farmers as promised. But one woman said the village authorities neither asked her permission nor told her of their decision to demolish her two family homesteads. She was in the dark until she found her home being flattened by a digger. When journalists came to investigate, the village chief warned her not to complain. She was relocated to a new home and given only US$230 for her loss. 'The village leaders forced me out of my home to build the new countryside,' she told the newspaper.

None of the farmers who lost their homes knew about Chongqing's experiment with *dipiao*, according to the report. Nor did they know how much the *dipiao* for their land had been auctioned for. 'The village authorities only said they were building the new countryside and if we agreed to leave our homes we would be given Rmb30,000 (US$4,500) compensation,' another villager told the newspaper. But when the money arrived, it was less than they had been promised. Villagers were also promised Rmb90,000 per hectare of land that was reclaimed, but only received Rmb60,000. Finally, they were told they could buy their new apartment for Rmb520 (US$80) per square metre, but actually had to pay Rmb650 (US$100). County officials insist that all the compensation was paid, which raises the question of who pocketed the money on the way.

It is impossible to know how widespread the abuses in Chongqing are, but policymakers in Beijing are clearly worried that the *dipiao* exchange gives corrupt officials a new way of stealing land. In December 2010, the State Council issued a notice promising to crack down on all land swaps initiated unilaterally by local governments. The central government warned that, while it remained broadly supportive of experiments in land and *hukou* reform, it would not countenance these reforms being used as a ruse for illegal land grabs.

So far, Chongqing's *dipiao* market has withstood the political pressure. But there will clearly be considerable opposition to extending Chongqing's land reforms nationwide. If land trading is carried out according to the law and farmers are properly compensated for their loss, it truly has the potential to revolutionize the rural economy. The problem, as ever, is China's murky political system and weak rule of law. As long as power remains concentrated in the hands of a few powerful individuals, with few checks or balances, abuses will inevitably occur.

城市化

Chongqing's land and *hukou* reforms are the country's most ambitious. But similar reforms – and, inevitably, similar abuses – are occurring across the country. Guangdong and Shaanxi are also experimenting with reforms to allow qualified farmers to exchange their land for permanent city residence. And many sub-provincial localities, especially smaller cities, let farmers swap their land-use rights for an urban *hukou*. Since Communist leaders passed the Resolution in 2008, there have been disappointingly few central government policies to promote land reform. Local governments have taken the lead. The problem, as the central government knows only too well, is that these piecemeal reforms provide enormous potential for corruption.

The Wukan incident shows only too clearly that land grabs can have serious consequences. Around 200,000 hectares of land are requisitioned from China's farmers every year, leaving some 3 million farmers landless and sparking an estimated 60 per cent of 'mass incidents' of social unrest. An estimated 40–50 million farmers have lost their land since local governments began to buy up vast tracts of farmland in the mid-1990s. If the number of landless farmers continues to grow, so too will the social instability they spread. More to the point, a seething mass of landless farmers could potentially threaten the Communist Party's grip on power.

The crux of the land problem is often couched in ideological terms: China's Communist hardliners will not countenance the privatization of collective land. But money may prove a bigger obstacle to reform. Undoubtedly, many land grabs in China are motivated by personal greed. Local officials want to get their hands on local farmland to sell on to developers for a lucrative profit. Villagers in Wukan claimed they were still waiting to be compensated for 400 hectares of land requisitioned since 1998, and accused local officials of pocketing more than US$100 million of compensation money since 2006. But other land grabs are motivated less by individual avarice than by local governments' desperate need to fill their bare coffers. Since agricultural taxes were abolished in 2006, this problem has only worsened.

What to do? Tao Ran, an expert on land reform at Renmin University, says the first task is to ensure that farmers are allowed to sell their land for its full market value. This would require cutting local officials out of the sales process and allowing farmers to negotiate with developers directly. Urban areas have a well-functioning land market with clearly defined land use rights, including strict regulations on land takings and compensation. So the long-term aim should be to introduce a unified land market, giving farmers the same rights to their land as urban homeowners have to their property. In its *China 2030* report, the World Bank agreed: 'China will need to reconsider the State's unique monopoly power in the primary land market which gives it the sole right to convert land for urban use and allow for the role of the State to be transformed into that of a market regulator, administrator and service provider, and enforcer of rules' (World Bank and DRC 2012: 136).

Clearly, giving farmers the right to sell their own land would mean huge losses to government revenues. But this loss, Tao argues, could be plugged by the introduction of new taxes on land sales and property. Farmers selling their own land would have to pay a tax to ensure that the public purse took its share of the capital gains. Second, China should introduce a property holding tax. Policymakers have long toyed with introducing an urban property tax, both to bring down soaring house prices and to provide city governments with a steady income not reliant on selling land. Almost all developed countries levy a property tax (known as Council Tax in the UK) to help finance local services. But so far, aside from limited pilot projects in Chongqing and Shanghai, China's leaders have ducked making this politically sensitive decision.

In February 2012, Wen Jiabao demanded better protection of farmers' land rights. During a visit to southern Guangdong, not far from Wukan, the Chinese premier criticized the 'arbitrary seizure of farmers' land'. A month later, at the annual meeting of China's parliament, Wen said the central government would help farmers register their land rights and set new rules ensuring they were compensated for any loss. 'These rights must not be violated by anyone,' he declared. These words followed Wen's earlier comments at the National Rural Work Conference in December 2011, when he vowed to let farmers benefit more from land sales, admitting that China had 'lowered the costs of industrialization and urbanization by sacrificing farmers' rights to land'. In the same month, Renmin University's Professor Tao wrote an op-ed for the *Guardian*, reflecting on the stand-off in Wukan. 'Wukan should be a signal for China to reform its land requisition system in order to keep local governments away from the financial gains of abusive land taking,' he argued (Tao 2011a).

If China's leaders have the guts and wherewithal to listen to their own experts, the country could yet find itself on the cusp of a third land revolution. Reforms in Chongqing and Chengdu show what could be gained by opening up the land to financial markets. If these reforms were rolled out nationwide, as some reports have suggested they may be, they could help to transform rural finance. Yet this cannot happen while farmers' rights are so open to abuse. Thirty years after the dissolution of the Maoist collectives, China stands at a crossroads: if leaders want their urbanization policies to succeed, they must reform collective land ownership, introduce private property rights, and ensure these rights are properly enforced. Unfortunately, it is very doubtful whether any of these reforms are possible under China's current political system.

BOX 3.2   The beginning of the end for traditional farming?

Read almost any article or watch any television report about China and you could be forgiven for thinking the country consisted only of teeming cities interspersed with factories. The media's urban bias fails to reflect the fact that, despite thirty years of industrial development, China remains a highly rural country. Even taking into account the 250 million or so rural migrants who have left home to find jobs in towns and cities, nearly half of China's citizens still live in rural communities. The average Chinese person is as likely to spend his days bent over a paddy field as he is working in a factory or sitting in an office. There are roughly 200 million farming families in China, and these rural folk remain poor.

Raising rural incomes is the holy grail of Chinese development policy, and no more so than in Chongqing, where rural incomes are a paltry 28 per cent of the urban average. Like other places in central China, Chongqing suffers from a massive rural labour surplus that limits the potential gains from farming. The average rural household farms an area just one-third the size of a football pitch, including land informally transferred to permanent rural residents from migrants working in the city. Conquering rural poverty will require reducing the number of farmers and consolidating the land so it can be farmed more efficiently.

Most farming families in Chongqing live a largely subsistence life, relying on family members who have left the fields to top up their incomes. Chongqing villagers now typically live in new two-storeyed homes with shining tiled walls, paid for by relatives working in the factories or on the building sites far away in the city. But this pattern of living off handouts from the urban economy may be about to change: just a few years after China's central leaders decided to encourage the transfer of rural land, a genuine market in farmland is beginning to emerge. Most land transfers are between farmers, but they also include transfers to agribusinesses looking to consolidate land, invest in better irrigation and machinery, and reap the benefits of scale.

Zhongdu village, which lies 130 kilometres northwest of Chongqing city, is one of seventy village collectives engaged in an experiment to raise local incomes and boost land productivity. Local farmers have leased out hundreds of hectares of land, clearing away individual family plots and replacing them with a huge field of cash crops. On a sunny spring afternoon, representatives of a Guangdong food company inspect hundreds of plots on which villagers grow food for the family table. Led around by the village chief, a stocky man sporting a spiky moustache and missing several front teeth, they negotiate a deal to lease the land and grow mass quantities of vegetables.

Half of Zhongdu's farmland has already been consolidated into one giant field filled with watermelons and vegetables, which grow in identical rows covered by transparent plastic sheeting pulled tight over arched bamboo poles. The field is lined with concrete ditches and watered by new wells. The project began in 2010 with a combination of public and private money: Rmb7 million (US$1 million) from the central government, Rmb4 million from the municipal government, and Rmb3 million from local businesspeople. The food company from Guangdong is eyeing up the other half of the village, which remains divided into a traditional patchwork of tiny plots.

Villagers receive annual rent of Rmb600 per *mu*, which works out as about US$750 per hectare. That is less than the average Rmb900 per *mu* recorded in 2010 by Tuliu.com, China's largest online platform for buying and selling land; but locals consider it a fair price. Some claim their cash income from farming before the project began was only Rmb1,000, but under the new system they can top up their rental income by working for a wage of Rmb30 a day, a little under US$5. Many of the farmers in the village are old, and living off the rental income is preferable to gruelling days spent sploshing around a paddy field. They say they were encouraged to rent out their land by the village chief, but not forced to do so. 'There's nothing feudal about it,' says one farmer. 'We're not worried about inviting in new landlords, because the land rights still belong to us.'

In the half of the village that remains divided into tiny household plots, the men from Guangdong spread out a map beside their flashy 4 × 4 vehicle. It is only a matter of time before these fields are cleared and put to more productive use. Traditional Chinese farming is fading away.

4

The Construction Orgy:
Paving the Fields

Since the early 1980s, the built-up area of China's cities has expanded more than fourfold. The vast swathe of concrete and asphalt that is modern urban China is now large enough to cover an area the size of Switzerland. On a broader measure of the urban area, which includes parks and economic zones, China's cities would cover an entire mid-sized country such as Syria or Cambodia. Over the past three decades, China's cities have been transformed by an orgy of building unleashed by market forces, but driven, too, by government officials satisfying their overwhelming craving for development. Beyond the nation's seedy karaoke parlours, nothing turns on a typical Chinese official more than a tangle of car-filled flyovers. In Mao's time, China's cities were dominated by factories and low-rise housing compounds; today they increasingly have the full gamut of shops, restaurants and offices, connected by endless grey ribbons of congested roads and filled with the residents of countless giant apartment blocks.

Even if China's urban population had not grown at all, the demand for larger homes, shopping malls and industrial parks would have pushed China's cities well beyond their existing boundaries. But during the past thirty years China's urban population jumped by 500 million. By 2030, China's cities are projected to swell by a further 300 million people. That figure is necessarily a rough estimate: any number of unpredictable events could potentially derail China's urbanization process. But if China can maintain its upward growth trajectory for the next decade or more – and both China's demographics and its moderate level of economic development suggest there is no reason why it should not – China's cities will have to expand further to accommodate the swarm of new urbanites.

China already contains some of the world's largest cities, and those cities must prepare to become still larger. Counting city populations is tricky, but Beijing, Shanghai, Shenzhen, Dongguan and Guangzhou-Foshan are already 'megacities' – defined as urban areas with populations in excess of 10 million – according to research by Demographia, an urban planning website. And current trends suggest that Tianjin, Shenyang, Wuhan, Chongqing and Chengdu could soon join them in the megacity rankings. As economic prosperity pushes inland, more migrants are choosing to move to cities closer to home, and urban powerhouses in the interior will attempt to match the prosperity of the coastal pacesetters. In addition, China has hundreds of smaller cities and big towns with populations below 1.5 million. The sheer size of China's rural population means that smaller cities, as well as megacities, will be needed to accommodate the influx of migrants from the countryside. If China's leaders can summon the political will to ensure that rural migrants are housed in modern apartments, rather than left to languish in slums and basements, the physical expansion of China's cities will continue apace.

城市化

Over the past decade, China did a remarkable job of housing its growing urban hordes. Its success can largely be attributed to the privatization of the housing market in the late 1990s. Until then, most urban residents lived in poky flats or dormitories provided by their state work units. The birth of the private property market created a new supply of bigger and better apartments, and sparked an explosion of demand among native urbanites to fill them. Giant skyscrapers and flashy opera houses make the headlines, but they are like the signature dishes at a Chinese banquet, designed to show off the wealth of the person paying. The plain bowls of white rice that fuel the country's construction industry are residential tower blocks. For ordinary citizens, access to bigger and better housing is the most revolutionary aspect of China's urban building boom.

The construction frenzy, however, has had a serious consequence: it has gobbled up field after field of precious farmland. China is using its most precious resource – land – far less efficiently than it needs to. China's urban land area is expanding much more rapidly than its urban population, and its cities are far less densely populated than they used to be. The built-up area of Chinese cities more than tripled to 40,000 square kilometres in 1980–2010, even though the urban population expanded by a much smaller 120 per cent. The urbanization of land, in other words, has far outpaced the urbanization of people. Living conditions have improved enormously, but at the expense of urban sprawl.

Policymakers fear that the loss of farmland could eventually threaten national food security. One solution is simply to import more produce, but that argument holds little water among leaders who grew up amid the famines of the 1960s. China remains determined to grow as much of what it eats as possible. So, as cities continue to expand, requisitioned farmland must be used more efficiently. Greater intensity of land use – which would require denser, more compact cities – would also generate huge savings in energy and construction materials.

Urban sprawl is worsening across the country, especially as new housing is built in the suburbs and people become increasingly dependent on cars. More and more cities are building to accommodate vehicles rather than people. This is important because one of the biggest factors in shaping the physical development of China's cities is road design, and poor road design can quickly scupper compact urban planning goals. Massive urban road-building programmes, coupled with the explosion in private car ownership, risk creating spread-out cities like Los Angeles. As more infrastructure springs up to serve suburban communities and growing car usage pushes city boundaries ever outward, the process of suburbanization is becoming self-reinforcing. 'Chinese cities are creating a pattern of development that is unfriendly to public transport,' says Shomik Mehndiratta, a transport specialist at the World Bank. 'Once you create this, it is hellish to fix.'

At the heart of the problem is China's dysfunctional fiscal system, which provides city governments with distorted incentives to expand the urban boundary. Most local governments in China run a perennial budget deficit, because they are required to provide more services than they can afford. To find enough cash, cities are forced to sell land. On average, one-quarter of local government revenue comes from land sales, but this figure can be considerably higher in some cities. This financial model is a major driver of China's housing and construction boom, yet it also provides a strong economic basis for continued urban sprawl.

The problem dates back to major reforms made to the tax system in 1994, part of wider fiscal reforms designed to shore up shrinking central government revenues. Reported government revenues fell from one-third of GDP in the late 1970s to just 10 per cent by 1995, as market reforms and greater competition from the private sector destroyed profits at state-owned enterprises. In the scramble to revive central revenue collections, the responsibility for financing costly public services such as education, health care and social welfare was assigned to local governments. Yet Beijing simultaneously required local governments to send most of the taxes they collected back to central coffers, thereby forcing them to pay for more public services from a much smaller funding pot. Central transfers help to fill the hole in local budgets, but the vast majority of local governments struggle to finance social spending. In the mid- to late 1990s, the sudden financial pressure imposed by these reforms was exacerbated both by the restructuring of township and village enterprises and by the bankruptcy of many local state-owned enterprises, which greatly increased local governments' social security burden. This left local governments with no choice but to develop their major natural resource: land.

The lucrative game of selling appropriated farmland to property developers means that local-government finances and urban planning have become intertwined. For example, using road projects to mandate the conversion of agricultural land for construction purposes is an easy way to meet development goals while simultaneously filling local coffers. This goes a long way to explaining officials' unwavering faith in the value of ring roads, which allow them to increase the potential area for urban development in one stroke, as all land within an orbital will quickly become fair game for development. Beijing, the worst offender, has five of them. 'What's the best way to take the land?' asks the World Bank's Mehndiratta. 'You draw a circle around the city and call it a ring road. It's the most efficient way of circumscribing rural land. This means you have all the incentives for urban sprawl.'

Roads and housing are to blame for the loss of huge swathes of farmland. Yet there is a still bigger culprit: industrial development. The hundreds of industrial zones found on the outskirts of China's cities, both big and small, are the most important cause of low-density sprawl in China's cities. Again, this problem dates back to the fiscal reforms of the mid-1990s. When localities lost much of their revenue stream in 1994, they began to fight one another for investment from manufacturers who could provide a future tax base. Even pint-sized cities began to build what became known as 'economic development zones'. These zones all look the same: a sprawl of low-rise factory or office buildings criss-crossed by empty roads, often up to ten lanes wide. Even if city centres remain bursting at the seams, vast areas of land on the urban fringe are wasted.

When local officials allocate a piece of land for an industrial zone, they work tirelessly to attract investors from all over the country. They offer an array of sweeteners, such as dirt-cheap rents and subsidized infrastructure, and may even relax labour and environmental protections. These policies are designed to maximize income from local governments' two principal revenue sources: land sales and taxes on industrial production. Local governments tightly control the supply of land for residential projects so they can make fat profits on high land prices. Yet they hand over vast tracts of cheap land for industrial projects so they can skim off the subsequent production tax revenues. Because localities earn revenue from taxing production value rather than profits – which, under the current fiscal system, are sent to Beijing – they are assured of a stable income even if the factories are only marginally profitable or even loss-making.

The result is that local governments have an incentive to offer up thousands of hectares of land to investors, many of whom are wealthy multinational companies, at rock-bottom prices. Tao Ran of Renmin University estimates that up to one-quarter of economic and industrial zones rent out land at less than half of its development cost. In the early 2000s, the cost of developing land for manufacturing in Suzhou ran to Rmb3 million (US$360,000) per hectare. But officials in Suzhou, consistently the biggest destination for foreign investment in China, decided to lease industrial land for a loss-making Rmb2.3 million. In a desperate race to the bottom, this forced less popular neighbouring cities to drop their prices still further, to as low as Rmb750,000 (US$90,000), as they struggled to compete.

The number of economic development zones grew so quickly during the late 1990s and early 2000s that the central government decided enough was enough. In 2003, a government survey found 6,866 zones around the country, occupying nearly 40,000 square kilometres of land. Beijing halted the approval of all new zones and set about whittling the number down to a more acceptable level. By 2006, there were 1,568 economic development zones left, occupying less than 10,000 square kilometres. This looked like a triumph for the central government, but enterprising local governments simply reopened most of the banned economic development zones under a new name. To this day, most Chinese cities are surrounded by 'industrial' or 'high-technology' zones, in addition to economic development zones. Despite the central government's best attempts, the area of land occupied by industrial zones has only increased.

The most egregious example in recent years is Liangjiang New Zone in Chongqing. Roughly twenty times the size of Manhattan Island, it is modelled on Shanghai's Pudong New Area. After just a decade of development in the 1990s and early 2000s, Pudong – located across the Huangpu River in eastern Shanghai – became one of China's largest financial and export-processing hubs. Opened with the approval of the State Council in 2010, Chongqing's leaders hope Liangjiang can replicate Pudong's success. The zone is a key part of Mayor Huang Qifan's plan to turn Chongqing into interior China's premier transport, manufacturing and finance hub. Liangjiang has its own state-of-the-art bonded port and includes special areas devoted to high-tech manufacturing, logistics, finance and 'eco-industry'. Dozens of villages have been bulldozed and hundreds of hectares of agricultural land flattened to realize Huang's expensive vision.

Nationwide, the extent of the problem is clear in the numbers. The area of land occupied by industry rose from 7,900 square kilometres in 2004 to 9,853 square kilometres by 2008 – more than one-quarter of all urban construction land. By comparison, the 31 per cent of land used for residential use is surprisingly low. The problem seems to be getting worse: industry gobbled up 45 per cent of all *new* urban construction land in 2006–08, while only 20 per cent was used for housing. And local governments continue to hand over land at ludicrously low prices: in 2010, the average price of land leased to industry was up to eight times lower than land leased for commercial and residential projects.

By effectively squeezing the supply of land for housing, local governments create a sellers' market for residential land and a buyers' market for industrial land. In 2008, residential land sales generated 58 per cent of total land sales revenue, compared to just 17 per cent from industrial land sales. The impact of price-ramping on China's house prices, which in expensive cities like Beijing can reach twenty times average income levels, is enormous. China's high house prices do not result simply from a scarcity of urban land, but from how local governments choose to use it. By squeezing the supply of residential land while simultaneously handing over cheap land to industry, local officials push up property prices, stoke industrial overcapacity, and waste millions of hectares of agricultural land. Over the past decade, this model of economic development was a major contributor to China's sizzling economic growth – but it also created economic imbalances and worrisome social problems.

One consequence of the distorted land market is that low-income families and first-time buyers find themselves locked out of the property market. As rising house prices make city centres unaffordable, these people have to move into cheaper accommodation in suburbs and satellite towns – further exacerbating urban sprawl. City governments are keen to maintain this outward flow, both to improve congestion in city centres and to shore up the market for new land. Both Shanghai and Beijing, for example, are attempting to lower the population density in their respective city centres. Just ten years ago, suburbs such as Shanghai's Baoshan or Beijing's Tongzhou were essentially satellites; today they have been absorbed into the city. The flight from the urban core is exacerbated by government attempts to convert high-density city centres into commercial districts, which often requires kicking the original residents out into the suburbs. Many cities further encourage urban sprawl – and deliberately try to ramp up land prices – by moving government offices and universities into the city outskirts.

Rural migration, especially in the big southern manufacturing towns of Guangdong and Zhejiang, adds to the physical expansion of China's cities. Many of these workers may only be temporary residents, but the dormitories, shops and roads built to accommodate them expand the urban boundary. Making land available for migrant housing is far less lucrative for city governments than selling it to developers to build plush residential complexes and shopping malls – but it allows cities to industrialize on the cheap, without having to pay for proper public housing. To take one extreme example, the built-up area of Dongguan, a manufacturing centre in the Pearl River Delta with a predominantly migrant population, expanded almost sixtyfold from 14 square kilometres in 1990 to nearly 800 square kilometres by 2010.

Beijingers sometimes compare the expansion of their city – an endless, sprawling flatness of roads, apartment blocks, wholesale markets and industrial zones – to making *jianbing*, a favourite local pancake. The process, normally performed by street vendors, involves pouring pancake dough onto the middle of a round, flat griddle. The vendor then scrapes the dough so that it expands to cover the entire surface of the griddle. As China runs out of farmland, it must find a way of keeping the *jianbing* effect under control.

城市化

China's wasteful pattern of development explains, in part, why international comparisons suggest that its cities are underpopulated. This sounds crazy: China's cities do not feel short of people. But of the 858 Chinese cities identified by a study by the McKinsey Global Institute, only thirteen have populations above 5 million (McKinsey Global Institute 2009a). This matters, because China has to feed one-fifth of the world's population with just 7 per cent of its arable land. Around 80 per cent of China's urban residents live in cities with a population below 5 million, similar to the figure in the United States, whose land resource per head is eight times greater. In Japan, which also suffers from a shortage of arable land, the figure is 45 per cent. If China had fewer small cities and more big cities, it could fit many more residents into a smaller area.

McKinsey's analysis, however, suggests that China is moving towards a largely dispersed model of urbanization. By 2025, the study predicts, China will develop a 'distributed' pattern of growth as more than a hundred new cities with populations of between 500,000 and 1.5 million mushroom across the country. They will be joined by a further sixty new mid-sized cities with populations of between

1.5 and 5 million. Current trends suggest that small and mid-sized cities will become the primary engines of economic growth. By 2025, McKinsey forecasts, 70 per cent of the urban population will live in urban areas with populations below 5 million, and these towns and cities will generate more than half of urban GDP.

McKinsey's analysts argue that this model of urban growth is wasteful and inefficient. They say it would be far more productive for China to pursue a more concentrated urban development model, with growth concentrated mainly in a smaller number of very large cities. They identify two possible models of concentrated urbanization: a 'super-cities' model built around fifteen cities with populations of 20 million, and a 'hub-and-spoke' model with clusters of smaller cities developing around larger ones. Both of these models, McKinsey estimates, would result in a considerably higher per-capita urban GDP than under the current distributed model.

This is an interesting argument, but the reality is that China is already well down the road to a pattern of mainly distributed urbanization, dominated by lots of small and medium-sized cities – albeit punctuated by the occasional megacity. Local officials across the country are keen to see townships grow into small cities that can act as service and consumer centres for local farmers, and it is too late to make any fundamental change to this pattern of urban development. In fact, the arithmetic of China's gigantic population makes a distributed model of growth almost inevitable. Even if China succeeds in creating twenty megacities of 30 million people by 2030, that will still leave another 400 million urban residents to be housed in smaller urban centres.

One reason for China's dispersed urban geography is that, since the late 1990s, successive governments have plumped fairly decisively for widespread urbanization on grounds of equity. It was widely viewed as unfair that China's coast hogged all the fruits of development in the 1980s and early 1990s – so the central government attempted to rebalance national development by ploughing huge funds into urban growth centres in the central and western hinterlands. The Great

Western Development Initiative, launched in 2000, pumped billions of dollars into developing infrastructure in China's least developed region. To some extent, this is an example of a well-entrenched Chinese policy habit of trading away efficiency to achieve more equitable distribution. But there is also an economic case: it may be that a comprehensive network of mid-sized cities blanketing the whole country will create a healthier and more stable domestic national consumer market than an archipelago of giant urban islands.

The latest government thinking has shifted in favour of bigger, denser cities. After years of promoting the growth of small cities and allowing large cities to sprawl ever outwards, policymakers now say they want to foster a more concentrated mode of urbanization. 'The current physical pattern of urbanization is unsustainable,' Yang Weimin, secretary general of the National Reform and Development Commission, China's national planning body, told a forum in Beijing in 2011. The central government has announced that future urban development will be built around five 'national central' cities – Beijing, Shanghai, Tianjin, Guangzhou and Chongqing – along with six 'regional central cities', Shenzhen, Nanjing, Wuhan, Shenyang, Chengdu and Xi'an. The 12th Five Year Plan identifies twenty designated centres for future urbanization, with the aim of directing growth into clusters of large cities. The idea is to form networks within each cluster, thereby creating a larger labour pool and preventing duplication of infrastructure.

Ostensibly, the principle of encouraging large cities to grow even larger makes economic sense: urban centres with concentrated populations create more jobs than smaller cities, and are cheaper to provide with goods and services. But there is a very real danger that the individual cities within these clusters will merge to create vast, unmanageable seas of concrete. Although megacities benefit from economies of scale, they can easily become intolerably congested and polluted. Economists and urban geographers disagree over the point at which the marginal cost of adding more residents exceeds the social benefits gained. McKinsey's researchers argue that there are no fixed limits beyond which cities cannot grow productively: 'The only hurdle to the growth of urban centres is an inability to keep pace with, and manage, their expansion' (McKinsey Global Institute 2011: 14).

Is China's decision to direct growth into urban clusters orbiting huge megacities a recipe for economies of scale or for urban dystopia? That will depend on how these new megacities are managed. Tokyo–Yokohama, the largest urban area in the world, has a population in excess of 35 million. But its people are healthy and well fed, the air tolerably clean, and the city's efficient subway system ensures that commuters arrive at work on time. Seoul–Incheon, which has a population of more than 20 million, has regenerated most of the slums that blighted it in the 1970s and 1980s. By contrast, Delhi – the world's second largest urban area by population – suffers from inadequate infrastructure and appalling social deprivation.

The encouraging news is that China's developmental trajectory is closer to that of Japan than of India. Both the Yangtze and Pearl River Deltas, respectively centred on Shanghai and Guangzhou, are well on their way to becoming megalopolises (chains or clusters of large urban areas), and could soon resemble Tokyo–Yokohama. Along the lower reaches of the Yangtze, improved transport links mean that Shanghai, Kunshan, Wuxi, Changzhou and Nanjing are rapidly merging into one. Ten years ago, the 300-kilometre journey from Shanghai to Nanjing took several hours; today high-speed trains whisk passengers to Jiangsu's capital in just 75 minutes. In the Pearl River Delta, planners are working on a US$320 billion project to mesh together nine cities with a combined population approaching 50 million. The scheme seeks to integrate transport, energy, water and telecommunications networks. An express train will link the Pearl megalopolis to nearby Hong Kong.

Other second- and third-tier cities will also benefit from growing substantially bigger, even if they are not placed within an emerging megalopolis. Aside from using energy more efficiently and reducing the loss of farmland, larger cities benefit from a strong centre of gravity: they are generally much better at attracting educated labour

---

BOX 4.1 Tier what?

There is no universally accepted breakdown of China's market tiers. The following is a useful rule of thumb:

1   The megacities of Beijing, Shanghai, Guangzhou and Shenzhen.
2   The forty-odd cities that are capitals of wealthier provinces or that lie in high-income areas along the east coast.
3   The forty-odd cities that are capitals of poorer provinces or have populations of more than 2 million people.
4   Cities of 1–2 million people.
5   Cities of fewer than 1 million people.
6   Rural townships.

Source: Fathom China.

---

and investment than smaller cities. They also do better at absorbing new technology and providing a nucleus for the development of business and industrial clusters. All of this stimulates higher economic growth. Equally important, most big Chinese cities are simply better managed than smaller cities. Yet none of this means that China's hundreds of existing small cities are going to disappear. Officials in towns and small cities will continue to fight for everything they can get, and many small cities will grow as local farmers move off the land.

After years of see-sawing policies on urban development, China appears set to follow a dual model of concentrated *and* distributed urbanization. This is almost unique. In other developing countries, the simple megacity model predominates: migrants overwhelmingly head for the big smoke, be it Manila, Mexico City or Bangkok. By contrast, China has around 700 small cities and big towns with populations below 1.5 million. India, with five big metropolitan areas and a plethora of mid-sized cities, is probably the only country with a chance to replicate China's dual urbanization model. This is not the most efficient pattern of urban development that China could pursue, but it is too late to change the facts on the ground.

BOX 4.2 Scrabbling to fill the city coffers:
the role of local government investment companies

Local governments in China are frequently vilified for stealing land from farmers and selling it on to developers for a massive profit. The greed of officials anxious for skim-offs is one explanation for this practice. But another is fiscal pressure: local governments have enormous expenditure requirements and scant budgetary resources. Without land, local governments would be unable to fund social services or finance vital investment in urban infrastructure.

In China's cities, municipal governments must fund nearly all social welfare services, including health and education, on top of most infrastructure spending. The first priority is to ensure that schools and hospitals remain open, even if that means selling appropriated farmland. Once social services are taken care of, there is often little money left for financing the kind of grand construction projects that help to get local officials promoted. So local governments have no option but to borrow the funds. But here they face a fundamental problem: local governments are neither allowed to borrow from banks nor to issue bonds.

Local governments therefore had to come up with an alternative way of financing infrastructure spending. Their solution was to set up financing platforms – conventionally termed local-government investment companies (LICs) – that can borrow and invest funds on their behalf. Land, once again, is the key. Local officials take a piece of land and inject it into the new company, which then uses it as collateral to secure a bank loan. LICs are government-owned but nominally independent, so they operate outside the municipal budget.

The oldest LICs, typically known as 'urban development and investment companies', are legitimate organizations that finance city infrastructure projects. The number and type of LICs proliferated over the past decade, however, as rural counties and even development zones decided to get a piece of the action. LICs of different stripes help to finance every type infrastructure project: highways, rural roads, railways, power plants, harbour facilities, irrigation systems. But they have been accused of working in cahoots with real-estate developers to push up land and property prices. Roughly 70 per cent of LICs operate at the county level, where finances are generally much weaker than in large cities.

Today there are more than 10,000 LICs. The number surged after the government endorsed the creation of new LICs in late 2008, in an effort to boost domestic investment as the global financial crisis hit demand for Chinese exports. In March 2009, China's central bank issued a notice encouraging local governments 'to establish LICs to absorb loans from banks to provide credit support for central investment projects'. The result was an orgy of lending by state-owned banks to LICs, which financed well over three-quarters of the stimulus projects begun in 2009 and 2010. But as worries grew about the rising level of local government debt, critics attacked LICs for encouraging financial mismanagement.

LICs are often described as a scam cooked up by local governments to circumvent rules that prevent them from borrowing. In other words, they are effectively used to hoodwink the central government. The reality is less scandalous. The LIC model was pioneered by the China Development Bank, China's largest policy bank, as a useful means of financing local infrastructure spending. Central-government policymakers, in other words, were involved from the start. And, far from encouraging irresponsible spending, the whole point was to force local governments to invest more responsibly. LICs borrow from banks at commercial rates, and they do not carry any central government guarantee.

The model proved highly successful until around 2008, when LICs began to take advantage of surging land prices to jack up their borrowing to unrealistic levels. When regulators took a closer look at banks' loan books, it turned out that some LICs had borrowed funds without any land assets with which to collateralize them, securing loans with nothing more than a government promise to repay. The problem only worsened in 2009, when many more stimulus loans were rushed through without adequate collateral.

By 2010 LIC borrowing was out of control, and Beijing finally had to take action. First it banned uncollateralized transactions backed solely by local guarantees. Then it ordered the closure of the most egregious offenders and instructed local governments to bring infrastructure projects back on budget. China's banking regulator estimated that LICs had loans outstanding of Rmb9.1 trillion (US$1.4 trillion) – a significant amount, but nowhere near as high as some of the more outlandish estimates. The clampdown seems to have stopped the rot: local government debt only rose by Rmb300 billion (US$50 billion) in 2011, implying that new lending to LICs basically dried up.

So what happens next? Some LICs have already had their loan terms extended, but about Rmb3.2 trillion in LIC loans will mature by 2015. Many are collateralized with land whose value began to fall in late 2011. Some smaller LICs are likely to go bust, which means lenders will take a hit to their balance sheets. If half of collateralized LIC loans and all uncollateralized loans turn bad, the total of bad loans in China's banking sector could reach nearly Rmb2 trillion (US$320 billion) by 2014, four times the figure at the end of 2011. This is a lot of money, but would only bring the non-performing loans ratio up to a still manageable 2.3 per cent.

LICs still have a role to play in local government finances, but they must be regulated tightly. Loan officers need to be more realistic about the potential value of future land sales when assessing LICs' loan applications. Land prices always have the potential to fall as well as rise – even if the huge demand for land created by the urbanization process means that long-term prices should continue to climb. In the final analysis, though, China needs to reform its fiscal system so that local governments are less dependent on land for making ends meet. In the first place, local governments should be allowed to issue bonds, as long as they are priced properly – and some cities are indeed set to issue bonds on a trial basis. But, most importantly, Beijing must ease the financial pressure on local governments, either by boosting fiscal transfers or by shouldering some of the social welfare burden itself.

Chengdu and Wuhan: hinterland dynamos

When Beijing launched its Great Western Development Initiative (*xibu dakaifa*) in 2000 – better known as the 'Go West' campaign – most of China's western hinterland remained desperately poor. Central China was barely more developed. Beijing's solution to the conundrum of how to push economic development into the impoverished interior was typically technocratic: pump huge funds into creating a regional 'dragon head' in Chongqing, funnel more cash into other large cities, and invest still more in a series of mammoth engineering projects. The immediate task was to create an efficient transport network across a remote and often inhospitable region that remained cut off from the rest of the country, with the goal of opening up China's continental economy to domestic trade – just as the booming cities of the eastern seaboard fed off markets overseas.

More than ten years on, this vision has largely been realized. China's wild western provinces are knitted together with new roads and railways. Central China is now within easy reach of the coast, thanks to the country's much maligned but truly impressive high-speed rail system. And the Yangtze, China's only natural transport artery into central and western China, is one of the busiest cargo rivers in the world. Multinationals have followed the infrastructure, establishing inland manufacturing bases to serve both foreign and domestic markets. The region's cities have been transformed from backwaters into thriving urban centres. Increasingly, they are home to a critical mass of consumers who demand, and expect, to live like their counterparts in Shanghai or Guangzhou.

The urban development in China's inland cities is awe-inspiring. As incomes rise across the country, China's building boom is spreading to places that few Chinese people could place on a map. As urbanization continues apace, more rural migrants will find work in cities closer to home, creating a more geographically balanced model of development. Policymakers are pinning the success of this urbanization process on a few poles of growth. In addition to Chongqing, two regional dynamos stand out for their potential to drive the urbanization process inland: Chengdu and Wuhan.

城市化

At first glance Chengdu, Sichuan's laid-back capital, looks like an advertisement for the long-awaited Chinese consumption boom. In the city's Louis Vuitton store, middle-aged businessmen with greasy comb-overs browse US$1,000 man bags, while their young mistresses ogle glittery gold sandals. With a 15-metre-high entrance illuminated by hundreds of flashing lights, the store is a beacon of bling in western China's most prosperous city.

Yet for all the tremendous progress Chengdu has made over the past decade, a more representative example of the local economy lies 75 kilometres away in the towering grey form of the Zipingpu Dam. Finished in 2006 with central government funds delivered under the Go West campaign, Zipingpu attracted unwanted column inches in May 2008 when cracks appeared following a massive earthquake in the nearby town of Wenchuan. The dam proved sturdy, but the huge reconstruction effort required after the earthquake, which killed more than 80,000 people, ensured that Sichuan remained a major recipient of central-government largesse. Chengdu, like Chongqing and Wuhan, is on its way to becoming a consumer centre, but it remains a big player in China's enormous building boom.

Chengdu sits at the heart of the Sichuan basin, a subtropical expanse of plains and low hills completely encircled by mountains, known as 'the land of abundance'. The basin's agricultural munificence nurtured some of the most advanced ancient civilizations in China, and Sichuan remains the west's grain and vegetable basket, as well as the country's biggest pork producer. But with a population that is overwhelmingly rural – Sichuan's urbanization ratio is around 40 per cent, ten points below the national average – the province as a whole is poor. Sichuan's cities are increasingly wealthy, but one in ten of its workers tries his or her luck elsewhere. Its population of 81 million is the same as Germany's, but its economy is less than one-tenth the size. Sichuan's GDP per head of US$2,500 is on a par with Egypt's, placing it in the bottom quartile of Chinese provinces.

Sichuan is a handy proxy for China's enormous hinterland. There are eighteen provinces in the officially designated central and western regions, which account for 55 per cent of national population but only 27 per cent of GDP. These hinterland economies depend not on the exports that drive the coast but on large-scale investments in urbanization, infrastructure and heavy industry. When the global financial crisis hit in 2008, coastal provinces were buffeted but Sichuan sailed through virtually unaffected – confounding foreign analysts who assumed an export slowdown would bring the entire country to its knees. Local economists say the investment boom must continue: they reckon that Sichuan is five years behind the nation as a whole and twenty years behind the most advanced cities of the coast.

Yet this strategy carries risks. With investment in fixed assets already accounting for more than 60 per cent of the provincial economy (and much of that investment financed by debt), Sichuan exemplifies the 'unbalanced' growth model that makes China sceptics wince. Beside every gleaming new office tower in downtown Chengdu sits a zombie high-rise from a building boom a decade ago. But a journey around the province confirms the stark fact that Sichuan needs more investment, and lots of it. Transport infrastructure is inadequate for the province's massive population and growing economy; and new factories, shops and apartment blocks are needed for the millions of rural migrants expected to move into the cities over the next two decades. This is the essential conundrum in China's growth model: China seems to have too much investment, but it needs so much more.

One only needs to travel along the expressway heading north from Chengdu to see where further spending is needed. Splintered glass and miles of twisted crash barriers testify to daily crashes on Sichuan's chief transport route, a jammed 100-kilometre highway that connects the province's three most economically productive cities – Chengdu, Deyang and Mianyang. On a typical morning, a bashed-up truck lists dangerously as it trundles along the inside lane. Ribbons of twisted metal flap around crates of broken beer bottles in its trailer. This is evidence of overcrowding, not just bad driving. When the two-lane expressway opened in 1994, Sichuan's economy was less than one-tenth of its present size. Since then traffic has exploded: the province has some of the highest passenger and freight volumes in China.

New roads and railways are badly needed to lighten the load. Fortunately, much of Sichuan's share of the economic stimulus spending that flooded the country in 2008–10 was directed into dozens of new transport infrastructure projects, including a new expressway between Chengdu and Mianyang and a high-speed rail line connecting Mianyang, Chengdu and Leshan, where tourists flock to see the world's largest reclining Buddha. These will come online soon. Another high-speed line between Chengdu and Chongqing, whose trains will cover the 309-kilometre distance in just 56 minutes, will take the pressure off the existing two-hour service.

Chengdu, like its competitor Chongqing, aims to become the transport and logistics hub of southwest China. Local officials say the city's new US$115 million railway container logistics centre is the largest in Asia. The centre will operate regular freight services to major coastal cities, slashing transport times and costs for exports of local goods. Sichuan's exports jumped nearly five times from US$6.6 billion in 2006 to US$29 billion in 2011, but still represented a puny 1.5 per cent of China's total. Sichuan's landlocked location means its primary focus will remain domestic trade. But Chengdu's Shuangliu airport has already established itself as the busiest passenger and cargo airport in central and western China, and there is plenty of room to boost exports of light, high-tech goods that can be economically shipped by air.

Sichuan's economy still relies on heavy industry such as petrochemicals, mining and metals smelting, transport equipment, electrical equipment and machinery. But increasingly the focus of Sichuan's industrialization push, especially in Chengdu, is on technology and light manufacturing – just the sort of labour-intensive industries that the rapidly growing city needs to provide jobs for thousands of migrant workers. Dozens of light manufacturers have moved to Sichuan from the coast to take advantage of lower costs and the growing domestic market, including a stream of contract manufacturers making shoes and furniture.

The province's biggest magnet for industrial investment is Chengdu High-Tech Zone, which occupies an entire district of the city and is reshaping its urban geography. More than 140 Fortune 500 companies have a presence in Chengdu, many of them here. The zone's biggest coup was persuading Intel to open a production plant in 2005, which led to subsequent investments by Semiconductor Manufacturing International Corporation (SMIC), the world's third-largest chip maker, and Molex, a US-based maker of electronic connectors and cables. Intel, IBM, AMD, Ericsson and Nokia all operate R&D centres in the zone, and Taiwanese contract electronics manufacturer Foxconn, which makes iPods and iPhones for Apple, has opened a US$800 million plant employing 100,000 people.

The zone, which sprawls across the southern and western suburbs, epitomizes Chengdu's helter-skelter urbanization process and is an excellent example of the wasteful expansion that blights so many of China's cities. It is leading a shift in the city's centre of gravity south: the municipal government moved its downtown offices there in 2010, and a new metro line running from the city centre is expected to lure thousands of new home buyers. Other development is moving in the opposite direction. The provincial government has relocated to the northwestern suburbs, partly to avoid the city centre's crippling traffic jams. And a new high-speed railway line to the small city of Dujiangyan, which lies 65 kilometres northwest of Chengdu proper but still within the municipal boundaries, should help a cluster of towns merge into a commuter corridor.

As Chengdu inexorably expands, meshing the urban and rural populations is a major policy challenge. In 2010, the city made headlines when an enterprising company began offering migrant workers accommodation in transport containers, nicknamed 'snail houses', for less than US$1 per night. So far, Chengdu's plan of freely handing urban rights to the municipality's 7 million rural residents has made little impact on people's daily lives. But successful integration of rural migrants is crucial for Sichuan – and, by extension, the rest of interior China – to move beyond the current growth model of state-led, debt-financed infrastructure investment overlaid with a thin veneer of Louis Vuitton glitz.

BOX 4.3   Riding the stimulus express

When a sleek express train glided into Dujiangyan's cavernous new railway station on 12 May 2010, central planners slapped each other on the back. Just two years to the day after a catastrophic earthquake crushed hundreds of children to death in Dujiangyan's shoddily built schools, the new 65-kilometre high-speed service from Chengdu provided a potent symbol of government-led renewal. The US$2 billion investment, Sichuan's largest single post-quake reconstruction project, was planned and built from scratch in just eighteen months. Like all of China's new fleet of high-speed trains, the Chengdu–Dujiangyan train is officially called the 'Harmony Express' – but a more apt name would be 'Stimulus Express'.

Sichuan was one of the biggest beneficiaries of China's enormous stimulus programme, which ran from late 2008 through 2010. Funds for quake reconstruction come out of the same funding pot as those for general stimulus projects. The magnitude-8 earthquake that ripped across western China on 12 May 2008 killed an estimated 87,000 people and left a further 15 million homeless. Officially, US$145 billion of Beijing's US$580 billion headline economic stimulus was ploughed into the three-year reconstruction process (the actual size of the stimulus was much greater).

Much of the cash was used for legitimate reconstruction. Just a few minutes from Dujiangyan's new station, children study in smart new schools, while thousands of local residents who lost their old homes have moved into blocks of attractive new apartments. But some of the funds were used to build projects, such as the Chengdu–Dujiangyan railway, that served no specific reconstructive purpose. Much of this extra investment, which neatly dovetails with wider government transport and urbanization policies, is useful. Yet there is also evidence of wasteful extravagance and financial mismanagement.

Dujiangyan, the nearest city to the epicentre of the earthquake in Wenchuan county, is the poster-child of the post-quake reconstruction effort. Dujiangyan is infamously associated with 'tofu schools' – cheap buildings that collapsed like soft cubes of bean curd when the earthquake struck, killing hundreds of children. Today the ancient city, once better known for its 2,000-year-old irrigation system than for its crumbling schools, buzzes with day-trippers from Chengdu. The downtown area, much of which was completely destroyed, has been totally rebuilt. A new expressway has cut the drive from Dujiangyan to Yingxiu, a small town in Wenchuan once reached by winding, mountain roads, to twenty minutes. Thanks to all the investment, locals say, Dujiangyan is more prosperous now than it was before the quake struck. The new train service, which brings Dujiangyan into Chengdu's commuter belt, has pushed up house prices, and the town's streets are snarled with shiny new cars.

Another example of successful reconstruction can be found 100 kilometres north of Chengdu in New Beichuan, where an entire county town has been built on requisitioned farmland. Around 20,000 residents were left homeless when the old town of Beichuan, located in a deep valley entirely ringed by mountains, was shaken to pieces by the quake and then flattened by landslides. New Beichuan, set alongside a river bank with a mountain backdrop, is the new capital of China's 200,000-strong Qiang minority, a matrilineal people who traditionally herded yaks and horses on the mountains of northwestern Sichuan. Spanning the river, a magnificent 150-metre bridge marks the entrance to a 'commercial town' of traditional-style Qiang buildings, carved out of stone and hewn from wood. Government planners view tourism as the route to rebuilding the area's shattered economy.

New Beichuan was built under a central government scheme,

known as *duikou*, which twinned different disaster zones with partner provinces and cities from China's rich east coast. Towns such as Beichuan (partnered by Shandong) and Dujiangyan (Shanghai) did extremely well out of the scheme, receiving lavish and thoughtfully planned investments. But charity workers say that the unstructured nature of the system, which gave partner provinces and cities huge leeway in managing the reconstruction process, created wide disparities in the recovery effort. The losers were millions of rural villagers, many of whom complained that the average US$3,000 subsidy they received fell well short of the US$10,000 cost of building a new home. Some farmers took out loans to make up the difference, but many were forced to dig into their life savings. Government policy clearly focused on urban development.

Another problem was mismanagement of funds. In some cases, officials redirected reconstruction cash to projects such as new roads or government offices; sometimes they simply stole the money. A five-month investigation by the National Audit Office of 72 major post-quake reconstruction projects in 2009 found that US$35 million of funds had been misappropriated. In the most outrageous case, in Mianyang, officials used US$20 million earmarked for the reconstruction of demolished homes to build a new district on the city's outskirts. Around 350 officials in Sichuan were hauled before their superiors for violating laws or Party discipline. Even charities were not immune: NGO workers suspect the Chinese Red Cross of paying off parents protesting over the loss of their children in 'tofu' schools.

It would be churlish to exaggerate the extent of these problems. Probably no other country could have mobilized so much capital and manpower so quickly and effectively: Dujianggyan and Beichuan were rebuilt within two years of the disaster. Yet it is worth pointing out that government planners used the reconstruction process as a cover for a series of wider economic policies that go much further than simply repairing people's shattered lives. Rebuilding Qiang villages as tourist destinations is designed to bring poor mountain folk into daily contact with the urban economy, while the construction of new towns and transport links tallies with the national urbanization drive. Sichuan's reconstruction is part and parcel of broader economic motives.

城市化

Wuhan, like Chongqing, has been called 'China's Chicago'. Like their American namesake, both cities are regional transport hubs with important river ports, making them gateways to the country's underdeveloped hinterland. And, like Chicago before them, both cities are being built on immigrants and their labour. More capital, both political and financial, has flowed to Chongqing – which also has a far superior record of producing Chicago-style gangsters. But Wuhan's geographical position at the very heart of China means it is probably better placed to serve the Chicago role.

Wuhan is one of a dozen Chinese cities expected to have a population in excess of 10 million by 2025. Depending on whom you talk to, the current figure is anywhere between 5 million and 10 million. 'We don't know exactly how many people are in Wuhan,' admits Zeng Juxin, professor of urban management at the city's Huazhong Normal University. 'The real city population is around 5 million, but rises to 8 million when you include all the permanent rural residents in the suburbs and surrounding countryside.' Add in a temporary population of up to 2 million – mainly college students and migrant workers from the surrounding central provinces of Hubei, Hunan, Henan, Jiangxi and Anhui – and the municipality is already home to 10 million.

Wuhan's central location makes it a magnet for migrants from all over the country. This includes temporary manual workers, but also long-term migrants looking for commercial and business opportunities. Growing numbers of local farmers are also moving into the city's outskirts, some clutching city *hukou* gained as compensation for having their land requisitioned. In addition, Wuhan is a major education centre, hosting more than 700,000 college-level students. Although graduates have traditionally left the city to find better-paid work nearer the coast, they are increasingly attracted by the growing local economy, especially in the batch of high-tech industries located on the southern fringe of Wuhan's attractive lakes area.

Controlling the city's expanding population is a major headache for the municipal government, which lacks the financial muscle of similarly large coastal cities like Guangzhou and Tianjin. Planning officials argue that the rising population is already putting too much pressure on the city's infrastructure, to the potential detriment of living standards. There is general agreement that the city proper cannot absorb more than 5 million residents, so further population growth will necessitate outward expansion. 'As the population grows, the pressure also grows to provide transport, employment and sanitation,' says Xie Wei of the Wuhan Housing Bureau. 'We need suburbs and satellite cities to take pressure off the city centre.'

In 2006, Wuhan launched a city plan for 2020 based on a hub-and-spoke model of urban development. According to the plan, the population of the city centre will be kept to 5 million, but the total population will rise to nearly 12 million. The majority of the city's residents will live in six residential spokes protruding from the city into surrounding fields, surrounded by 'hills and water'. The plan envisages suburbanites living and working on the city's outskirts without needing to commute into the centre, although every suburb will also be linked to the urban core by expressway and rail. In addition, new transport links will bring half a dozen smaller satellite cities into Wuhan's economic orbit, enabling some Wuhan residents to move out of the city and commute to work – a classic hub-and-spoke megacity model.

The plan includes strict regulations to prevent urban sprawl and protect the suburban greenbelt, plus zoning and density targets, varying according to area and property type, to keep the urbanized areas compact. 'We do not want limitless urbanization and industrialization; we need to control the spread of the city,' says Ying Yi, head of Wuhan's urban planning department. But Ying, who admits the plan will be 'hard to implement', says 'flexibility' will be allowed for extra expansion where it is needed. This raises the prospect that, for all the government's laudable aim to prevent urban sprawl, Wuhan's satellite cities will eventually merge with its suburbs to form a giant megacity. 'It will be impossible to control the spread of the city as the population expands,' warns Luo Jing, director of Huazhong Normal University's College of Urban and Environmental Science.

One of those areas can be found at the city's northern edge, where the towering smokestacks of Wuhan Iron and Steel loom behind bent-backed farmers tending vegetable patches. Today Qingshan district is a patchwork of tiny fields, polluted streams and roadside markets selling building materials. But the city government is in the process of transforming this no-man's-land into a sparkling new suburb. Between the steelworks and the mighty Yangtze River, demolished buildings and hoardings advertise a new logistics centre. Down the road, a giant railway station (Wuhan's third) and a 6-kilometre bridge (the city's fifth to cross the Yangtze) were completed in 2010. By the riverbank, where freshly planted grass lies forlornly under a fine layer of grey dust, workmen hammer at apartment blocks for the suburb's new residents.

Constructing a modern city centre and viable commercial hub, not to mention new suburbs and transport links, requires an enormous investment in infrastructure. This is especially true in Wuhan, whose position at the confluence of the Yangtze and Han rivers requires a further outlay on bridges and tunnels to relieve traffic bottlenecks between the three old towns of Hankou, Hanyang and Wuchang that constitute the modern city. 'Future development comes from investing in infrastructure first,' says Chen Juxin, vice-secretary of Wuhan Finance Bureau. 'We do not want to be like India,' he adds, pointedly.

Wuhan is working hard to catch up with the infrastructure and living standards of wealthier coastal cities, with large swathes of the city under reconstruction. In 2005, only 50 per cent of the city's wastewater was treated; by 2010 that figure exceeded 80 per cent. A massive house-building programme has boosted average living space to 30 square metres per head, an increase of more than 10 square metres over the past decade. The city's first tunnel under the Yangtze opened to traffic in 2009, followed by a new 5 kilometre road and rail bridge in Qingshan, which cost US$1.6 billion to build. In the same year, the country's first high-speed rail line opened between Wuhan and Guangzhou, carrying passengers nearly 1,000 kilometres in just three hours.

Yet keeping up with population growth and the heady speed of development is an almost impossible task. The number of vehicles on Wuhan's roads exceeded 1 million in 2010. This is just one-fifth of the total in Beijing, where traffic has reached preposterous levels, but city planners are struggling to keep up. 'The pace of new road planning and construction cannot match the growth of new cars,' says Cai Jing, deputy head of Wuhan police transport department. 'Often we need to make changes to a road as soon as the planners and the construction company have completed it.'

Officials say public transport is a priority to reduce chronic road congestion. Wuhan opened the first line of a new metro system in 2004, making it the fifth city in the country to have a subway after Beijing, Tianjin, Shanghai and Guangzhou. A second line should open in 2012, and a third has been approved for construction. One problem is making mass transit attractive to a public that increasingly aspires to private car ownership. Although Wuhan's public transport stacks up favourably against many cities in China, it is used by barely more than one-quarter of the city population – a figure the government hopes to push up to 45 per cent by 2020. 'Public transport is seen, to put it frankly, as poor people's transport,' says Zhang Jianwu, director of transport engineering at the Wuhan Transportation Science Research Institute. 'People think that if they take public transport, they'll lose face. But unless white collar workers and professionals choose to use it, it will be a failure.'

Perhaps the biggest sticking point, however, is financial. Although local governments are technically prohibited from borrowing, they all do so in practice via local-government investment companies, which are only nominally independent. Chen Juxin of Wuhan's

Finance Bureau says the city's LICs use future income streams earned from infrastructure projects as collateral for bank loans. All loans, he insists, must be paid back. In addition, the central government helps to finance large infrastructure projects; both Wuhan's new railway station and new bridge were partly paid for from central funds. 'The city government used to be very short of cash, but the situation is much better than before,' says Chen. 'The financial pressure remains intense, but we can now afford to invest in a lot of infrastructure projects that we could not in the past.'

From a financial point of view, channelling funds into steel and cement is considerably less daunting than addressing the much thornier issue of social security. Building new schools and hospitals is one thing; paying for pensions is another. Despite widespread migration, officials say the *hukou* system retains an important function for preventing farm families from moving en masse into cities. A huge influx of migrants demanding full social security could financially cripple large cities like Wuhan. 'Instead we are investing in rural infrastructure and services so that farmers do not need or want to move to the city,' says Chen, who admits that providing social security for urban residents is the city government's toughest task.

But as more and more migrant workers begin to settle permanently in cities, the demand for fair treatment and equitable access to social services will grow. This intractable problem is not addressed by Wuhan's plan for 2020. 'If there is no social security network for these people, the city will be unstable,' says Professor Zeng. 'We need to sort out the *hukou* issue, but no one knows what to do about it.'

BOX 4.4 Home, sweet home

Crossing over Wuhan's Han River gives a view of tumbledown housing as decrepit as anything in urban China. But Wuhan, like hundreds of other cities in China, is engaged in a monumental effort to give urban residents a decent place to live. All over the city, old apartments are being bulldozed to make way for higher-quality residential compounds, including subsidized 'social' housing.

One example is the Huangpu Renjia 'economic' housing complex in north Hankou, where flats are bought by lower-income families at below-market rates. The complex, which stands on the grounds of a demolished factory, is an oasis amid a sea of squalid tenements – freshly painted in fresh colours, with a large goldfish pond, tree-lined garden and children's playground. Retired residents sit in the garden or sip tea on their balconies. It is a far cry from the grey concrete housing blocks outside, with their grimy, open staircases. According to the residence manager, 40 of the 768 households who live at the complex receive the government's minimum living allowance, known as *dibao*. Every economic housing project in the city must provide a proportion of apartments to the poorest families, which the government rents out at a subsidized rate.

Tang Yonghua, a divorced woman in her fifties, moved into a new apartment in the Huangpu complex with her mentally disabled daughter in 2006. She pays rent of just US$5 per month for a 60-square-metre, two-bedroom apartment. 'You can't compare our new home to where we used to live; this is heaven for us,' she says, gesturing to the light and airy rooms with a view onto a pleasant courtyard. Her old flat, which she had to share with another family, cost four times as much and had no private bathroom. 'Lots and lots of people queued up to receive new apartments, so we were very lucky,' she says. 'But I believe that everyone will live in a place like this eventually. Society is progressing.'

5

Ghost Towns in the Desert: How China Builds Its Cities

'My name is Ozymandias, king of kings:
Look on my works, ye Mighty, and despair!'
Nothing beside remains. Round the decay
Of that colossal wreck, boundless and bare
The lone and level sands stretch far away.

Percy Bysshe Shelley, 'Ozymandias' (1818)

It is safe to assume that government officials in Ordos did not read Shelley's great sonnet 'Ozymandias' before they built a gleaming new city in the middle of the Gobi Desert. Shelley's poem was inspired by the fallen empire of Ramesses the Great, pharaoh of ancient Egypt in the thirteenth century BC. Ordos is a municipality in Inner Mongolia, not the capital of a great empire. But it does claim one-sixth of China's proven coal reserves, and this means it is very rich. Like Ozymandias, ambitious local leaders are building a great city in the sand.

Kangbashi New District, as it is known, features lavish public buildings and bucketloads of local pride. The municipal government's huge new headquarters overlook an enormous flagstoned square dotted with vast sculptures of Genghis Khan and his ravaging Mongol hordes. When Premier Wen Jiabao visited, locals say, he told officials their building was more luxurious than the Great Hall of the People in Beijing. Beside the square is an US$80 million museum, whose asymmetric exterior looks like a deformed UFO, and a US$60 million theatre, reminiscent of a traditional Mongolian cap sculpted in stone. An eight-storey public library features a glass-roofed courtyard and a floor reserved for Mongolian literature. Beyond the square, a sprinkling of skyscrapers and thousands of regimented apartment blocks shimmer under the desert sun. It is all very impressive, until you notice that the city is missing something essential – people.

Ordos is the poster-child of critics who argue that China's urbanization process has become unmoored from reality. In 2010, legendary short-seller and hedge-fund manager Jim Chanos proclaimed that China was on 'a treadmill to hell' (forgetting, it seems, that the whole point of treadmills is that they *don't* go anywhere) (Bloomberg 2010). Comparing China's reliance on property development to a heroin addiction, he declared that China's reckless investment practices were a bubble waiting to burst. A year later, doom-monger extraordinaire Nouriel Roubini, who anticipated 2008's global financial meltdown, warned that China's excessive investment rate could result in a financial crisis, years of anaemic growth, or both. Roubini cited the proliferation of 'ghost towns' – empty new cities – as evidence that China's excessive investment had crossed a critical threshold (McKeigue 2011). He was almost certainly thinking of China's infamous ghost town in the desert.

So are Ordos's leaders inflating a crazy bubble, or is there method in their madness? The local government drew up the blueprint for Kangbashi when Ordos's commodity boom took off in 2002. Money was no object: in 2006–10, annual GDP growth averaged a scorching 23 per cent and local government revenues jumped sevenfold over the previous five-year period, surpassing Rmb150 billion – well over US$20 billion. Per-capita GDP soared past US$20,000, twice the level in Beijing. The local government's idea was to kill two birds with one stone: to build a new town to house the municipality's growing urban population and to persuade wealthy locals to spend their money at home. Ordos's urban population jumped by more than 400,000 to 1 million in the first decade of the century, and is expected to keep growing. Kangbashi is designed to accommodate 300,000 people, a city the size of Newcastle-upon-Tyne or Pittsburgh. But officials were also keen to avoid the fate of neighbouring Shanxi, whose own coal bosses are famous for taking their money out of the province and spending their bags of cash on luxury apartments in Beijing.

The government's policy has been half-successful: the vast majority of Kangbashi's homes have local owners – yet up to 80 per cent stand empty. Most investors in the new city do not live there, instead preferring to remain in the old city of Dongsheng. Every morning, hundreds of government officials and employees of state-owned enterprises make the thirty-minute drive from Dongsheng through sandy scrubland to their shiny new offices in Kangbashi. In the evening they return to their homes in the bustling old neighbourhoods, where there are restaurants, shops and life.

Government planners say they chose this inconvenient location for the new city because Dongsheng is chronically short of water, whereas Kangbashi sits on the banks of a river. As Kangbashi develops and Ordos's urban population expands, they hope that more people will choose to move into the new city. Officials plan to move 150,000 farmers off the land by 2015, and these people will need housing. With compensation rates for some demolished homesteads on the edge of the city reportedly reaching up to US$300,000, many new urban residents will be able to afford to buy a home. In addition, Ordos is likely to attract thousands of urban migrants drawn by its boomtown credentials. Yet it remains far from certain that these new residents will choose to live in Kangbashi rather than Dongsheng, which is enjoying a construction boom of its own.

To planners' dismay, much of the private cash in Ordos is flowing into the water-starved old city. Dongsheng's skyline is filled with cranes, and its roads are congested with luxury cars. Dongsheng more closely resembles a resource-rich Middle Eastern mini-state than a typical Chinese city. Locals drive imported Range Rovers at US$250,000 each, and the pavements outside the city's glitzy karaoke halls are lined with Lexus SUVs. Taxi drivers claim they earn up to US$3,000 per month – six times the going rate in Beijing. Many of the locals walking along Dongsheng's drab but bustling streets are not long removed from the farm, but their leather clutch purses are stuffed with cash.

Ordos's new rich demand a luxury apartment along with a fancy car. 'Our customers are mainly coal bosses who have sold their business to the government or they've got rich doing property financing,' explains Ma Shaohua, a Beijing native and client manager at Prince Mansion, the swankiest new address in the old town. The 700-unit complex, which features marble floors and faux-baroque styling, is set in tree-lined gardens next to a bubbling river, until recently a stinking sewer. More than 150 of the 180 first-phase units sold within seven months of going on sale, despite a price tag of US$2 million each. 'They have the Louis Vuitton and the Armani, and now they want a luxury home and a luxury car – a Range Rover, Bentley or Rolls Royce,' says Ma.

Until recently, many of the city's inhabitants were not dissimilar from the people now building them their marbled palaces. In the centre of town, migrant workers take a break by the side of the road after a twelve-hour day lugging breezeblocks and pouring cement. They live in a filthy row of old village-style housing backing onto their construction site. Mr Zhen, a 54-year-old farmer from north central China, says this is his first stint as a migrant worker. 'Did you come to see the great western construction boom?' he asks cheerfully. Zhen earns US$450 a month working as a builder, a huge sum for a farmer and substantially more than most migrant workers around the country. 'People here used to be poor like me,' he says without resentment. 'But Ordos has exploded with wealth.'

For the moment, there are many more winners than losers from Ordos's commodity boom. The question is how long this can continue. At the end of 2011, reports suggested that Ordos's speculation-fuelled economy was beginning to unravel as local house prices dropped by up to a third. Sad tales emerged of amateur financiers and their borrowers committing suicide. When bubbles burst, it is a painful business. But Ordos can probably survive a market correction or two: the city has so much coal that both government officials and investors alike can afford to throw money at dubious construction projects for years to come. In any case, if Ordos's gamble fails, it has little relevance for the vast majority of property developments across the country. Most of these are new suburbs attached to existing cities, not mini-Dubais in the desert. Kangbashi will not slip into the boundless sands just yet.

There are even signs that the city in the desert is beginning to attract residents. On a busy strip of restaurants not far from the main square, the owner of a packed Sichuan eatery says business picked up considerably in 2011. More businesses are moving into the new city, and two university campuses have opened, bringing with them thousands of students. As Kangbashi's impressive new schools also open their doors, families will be attracted to the area, where house prices are lower than in Dongsheng. Mr Suo, a retired soldier who moved from the old town in 2009, says he was lured by cleaner air, space and cheaper prices. 'It's still pretty quiet, but we now have about a hundred households living in our compound,' he says. 'Back in 2009 Kangbashi *was* a ghost town, but not any more.'

城市化

Sorting fact from fiction in China's property market is tough. When stories about China's 'ghost towns' emerged in late 2009, the markets began to swirl with exaggerated rumours about the extent of over-building across the country. One popular claim, amplified by the market's echo chamber effect, was that China had 65 million apartments sitting empty. Suddenly every city looked like Ordos.

It is hardly surprising that China's property market is rife with rumour. Many of the biggest players in Chinese real estate are state-owned and unlisted, and around half of all property developments in China are not even sold on the open market. China's property-market statistics are contradictory and notoriously hard to interpret. To describe the market as 'opaque' does not do it justice. Yet the property market matters. China's economy, with its concentration of steel mills and cement plants, is unusually dependent on its construction sector. And China plays such an important role in setting prices for any number of raw materials that even a mild slowdown in its construction sector causes ripples across global commodity markets. If China's housing market really is one giant bubble, the world needs to know.

Fortunately, the investment gurus who propagate the 'China bubble' thesis are wrong because they misunderstand the nature of Chinese urbanization. They fail to comprehend its scale, and they base too many of their conclusions on business norms in the West rather than on those in China. Critics such as Jim Chanos and Nouriel Roubini are right that China's economic model encourages overinvestment and that its cities are littered with waste, but China's economy remains at a stage in its development at which efficiency is not the be-all and end-all. It can digest a few white elephants. Moreover, the truth of the matter is that China is not building too many apartments, and a handful of empty urban districts are not evidence of a giant property bubble. Chinese property investment may be inefficient, but it is sustained by a huge, growing and sustainable demand for new housing.

Most critics of China's property market fail to understand just how much new housing China's urbanization process will require. Every year, China's cities must absorb more than 20 million new inhabitants. In addition, as China's existing urbanites grow richer, they are demanding bigger and better apartments. In 2011, demand for new housing reached more than 10 million units, which should prove a sustainable number for the next decade or more. China's current modern housing stock, defined as homes with individual bathrooms and kitchens, is around 150 million units. But 200 million migrant workers currently live in dormitories or slum housing. If one believes that the urban poor deserve to live in proper flats, the corollary is that Chinese cities actually have a significant shortage of housing – somewhere in the region of 70 million units. China is not building too many new apartments; it is building too few.

As China grows richer, migrant workers and working-class urbanites will need to be rehoused in civilized accommodation. China's vast social housing programme, which began in earnest in 2009, represents the start of this process. GK Dragonomics estimates that 40–50 million new urban households will need to be housed between 2010 and 2020, while the total underlying housing demand for the next twenty years, including demand from upgrading and public housing projects, will be approximately 10 million units per year. Ill-conceived projects will fail along the way, and some developers and investors will lose money. But China's cities must build ahead to accommodate millions of new urbanites, and it makes sense to house people in new districts rather than hope that congested old neighbourhoods can bear the strain.

Most of these new districts will be built on the edge of expanding cities. The 'ghost towns' moniker is unhelpful because it implies that China is building lots of empty new cities. This is not the case: genuinely new cities are the exception not the rule. It is far more accurate to think of housing developments as new suburbs or satellites of existing urban centres rather than as orphans sprouting in the countryside. These suburbs provide much-needed housing for people relocating from older, smaller homes in the city centre and for young families looking for affordable homes. Most 'ghost towns' are merely new suburbs that people have not moved into yet. In time, China's empty cities will fill up.

城市化

Kangbashi in Ordos is a rare example of a genuinely new city. Three far more representative examples of new urban development can be found in the cities of Linyi, in the coastal province of Shandong; in

Zhengzhou, the capital of central Henan province; and in Kunming, the capital of Yunnan province in China's subtropical southwest.

Linyi is an unremarkable prefecture-level city once known for its sprawling wholesale markets but now better known for its abuse of the blind human rights activist Chen Guangcheng. Back in 2002, Linyi city had a modest population of 650,000. This made it little more than a large town by Chinese standards, and tiny compared with Shandong's major cities, Jinan and Qingdao. Yet Linyi city is the capital of an administrative unit containing many smaller towns and villages with a population in excess of 10 million, the largest in Shandong. One of those villages is Dongshigu, where Chen was held under illegal house after exposing forced abortions and sterilizations in his rural community. Aside from policing China's harsh family-planning policies, Linyi's government officials are promoted for boosting economic development. So in 2003 they set out to leverage their chief asset – a large but mainly rural population – and transform their sleepy town into a thriving metropolis.

Linyi's officials couched their plan in the politically correct language of 'urban–rural integration'. In reality, as in the urbanization drives in Chongqing and Chengdu, that meant moving farmers off their land and turning them into urban citizens. The government demolished rural homesteads, reclaimed and consolidated rural construction land for agriculture, and concentrated the ex-farmers in new urban neighbourhoods. In 2010, Linyi combined twenty-four villages into five city neighbourhoods that took up just 30 per cent of the space occupied by their old homes. The extra land created by this consolidation was either sold for urban development or used as collateral for bank loans to pay for building new homes and roads.

Linyi's total urban population, which includes a dozen or so smaller towns and cities in addition to the prefecture capital, jumped from 3.3 million in 2003 to 5.3 million in 2009, pushing the urbanization ratio up from 33 per cent to 48 per cent. Linyi city itself doubled in size to 1.5 million, and its urbanized land area nearly trebled. Local officials say they demolished and renovated 20 million square metres of urban housing in 2004-08 – enough to rehouse roughly 1 million residents – and built a further 1.8 million square metres of publicly subsidized 'economic' housing. They claim that 213,000 former farmers found urban jobs in 2008 alone, many as couriers in Linyi's wholesale markets. From 2003 to 2010, Linyi's pace of urbanization was a brisk 2 percentage points per year, faster than the national average.

Over the coming decade, city planners are preparing to move a further 2 million farmers into urban areas. Their aim is to push the prefecture's urbanization ratio up to 65 per cent. By 2020, they expect the total urban population to rise to 7.6 million, of whom nearly 3 million residents will live in Linyi city. The rest of the new urban population will move to twelve satellite towns, whose current populations of 100-200,000 are expected to double.

This ambitious plan presents the city government with a number of challenges. The first is to build sufficient homes and infrastructure to accommodate a fresh wave of migrants. Officials have focused this effort on constructing a new city district that faces the old city from across the banks of the Yi River, an expansive waterway lined with sandy beaches where locals swim in the summer. Nanfang New Zone, as the district is called, features wide roads, new schools, and a museum dedicated to science and technology. Many of the gleaming buildings would not look out of place in Shanghai: Linyi Commercial Bank, for example, occupies a forty-storey skyscraper. Inevitably, there is a huge new headquarters for the city government, which overlooks a mammoth public square and landscaped park, complete with an artificial lake spanned by traditional Chinese bridges. Yet five years after work began on the new district, the hundreds of apartment blocks and smart office buildings were unoccupied. Shops, restaurants and businesses were conspicuous by their absence. Like Kangbashi, all that was missing was people.

Driving through the vacant streets it is easy to conclude that Nanfang is an empty monument to the ambition of local officials

– a vanity project and a colossal waste of money. Officials may have the power to drive millions of farmers off their land, but they do not understand market reality. Some of the new apartment blocks are designated for expropriated farmers and employees of local state-owned enterprises, but most are for sale. Whether Linyi's local economy can create enough wealth and, therefore, demand to fill hundreds of thousands of empty flats is far from certain. The market rationale for Nanfang's shiny new buildings is speculative at best.

Yet the reality, as so often the case in China, may not follow conventional economic logic. Viewed from the local government's perspective, the new zone is a rational investment. Having already demonstrated that they can deliver rapid urbanization, Linyi's officials are justifiably confident they can hit their ambitious urbanization targets for 2020. And rather than building low-end flats on the outskirts of town to house incoming migrants (the cheaper alternative), it makes sense to invest in a pleasant new district where existing urbanites will want to live. Roughly half of nationwide demand for new flats is driven by existing homeowners looking to upgrade. When Linyi's upgraders move out of their old flats, less wealthy residents – including new migrants – can move in. Until then, the state-owned banks which helped to finance the investment can wait to get their money back.

Five hundred kilometres west of Linyi is Zhengzhou, one of the biggest cities in central China. Zhengzhou's new district, Zhengdong New Area, is so large that city officials had to gain approval from Beijing before building it. Officials in Zhengzhou, like Ordos, have received a barrage of criticism for their ambitious, and extremely expensive, project. Construction on the 115-square-kilometre site, which contains a business district, new headquarters for the provincial government, high-speed rail transport hub and fifteen university campuses, began in 2003. Total investment is reportedly expected to top Rmb100 billion. In December 2010, Zhengdong was featured in a report by US-based financial website *Business Insider*, which presented satellite images of Kangbashi and several other Chinese 'ghost cities'. The photographs of Zhengdong showed hundreds of empty new apartment blocks and public buildings.

Once again, not all of the criticism is justified. Zhengdong is designed to give Zhengzhou – the commercial centre of a teeming province with a population of 94 million – the modern infrastructure it needs to expand effectively. Already severely congested, Zhengzhou is home to around 11 million people, of whom nearly 6 million live in the city proper. Unlike Kangbashi, Zhengdong is an extension of the old city, to which it will soon be linked by the city's first subway line. When the satellite photographs of this new district were taken, it was hardly surprising that the public buildings looked empty: many of them had yet to open. In the summer of 2011, Zhengdong remained a work in progress, yet residential areas that had opened four or five years beforehand were filled with cars and people. Most brand-new apartment blocks were empty, but older neighbourhoods were thriving.

It is a similar story in Kunming, which has built a new district 20 kilometres south of the old city centre. Chenggong New District earned the distinction of being cited by the *Financial Times* in a discussion of China's investment bubble. But like Kangbashi, Nanfang and Zhengdong, Chenggong was not built on a whim during China's economic stimulus period of 2008–10 – a common criticism of much investment at that time. Kunming's resident population grew by 1.5 million in 2000–10, and the characterful city is determined to catch up with more developed cities along the east coast. The provincial Standing Committee planned the construction of a modern district to serve as a new centre for government, education and logistics back in 2003. If the plan works, Chenggong will house 950,000 people by 2020.

Government officials and university students will form the residential core of the new district. The city government has moved into its plush new headquarters, and nine university campuses are relocating from the old city. Down the road from Yunnan University's imposing new campus, salespeople at a residential compound say that 90 per cent of the apartments have been sold – some to investors, but most to university teachers. Prices here are one-third cheaper than in the old city. And the area is slowly coming to life, with restaurants and shops occupying around 30 per cent of the ground-floor commercial areas.

Chenggong, like thousands of new developments across China, is visibly wasteful. Chinese officials' obsession with gigantism ensures that city avenues, as Beijingers sadly discovered in 1989, are wide enough for a squadron of tanks to rumble down them. But the crucial question is whether these 'ghost towns' will remain empty. Both urbanization data and experience suggest that they have a good chance of filling up. Hundreds of once-empty districts across the country, from Shangdi in northwest Beijing to Donghu in southeast Wuhan, have turned into flourishing neighbourhoods. China's economic model, which relies on cheap financing and significant investment from the state, is wasteful. But there is far more slack in the system than in Western countries, which tend to value efficiency and immediate economic returns above anything else.

城市化

One example above all others shows how the Chinese model can work: Pudong. Shanghai's unlovely new district, built on the marshy banks of the Huangpu River, is the model for new districts nationwide. In 2011, Kangbashi (Ordos), Nanfang (Linyi), Zhengdong (Zhengzhou) and Chenggong (Kunming) were at much the same stage in their development as Pudong in 1998, when a visiting Milton Friedman slammed Shanghai's glittering new business district as 'a statist monument for a dead pharaoh on the level of the pyramids'. With the occupancy rate in its swanky new office towers at just 35 per cent, Pudong was itself something of a ghost town back in the late 1990s. Yet within a decade, Pudong's skyscrapers were full and millions of residents had moved into new homes across the Huangpu River. Pudong offers a lesson in patience: new districts must be given time to become viable commercial centres.

Friedman criticized Pudong as 'not a manifestation of the market economy'. Pudong was indeed planned by technocrats rather than commercial developers. But that provided a platform for its success: as private investors backed out or scaled down their plans, state-owned developers with deep credit lines remained patient. This gave Pudong enough breathing space to ride out its initial difficulties and emerge triumphant a few years later. The Shanghai government helped the process by instructing all the big banks to move their city headquarters to Pudong's new business district in Lujiazui. Few people at the time wanted to work in a sterile construction zone devoid of restaurants or greenery, but the government gave them no choice.

Now, there is no iron rule that other new districts will succeed like Pudong. Shanghai, after all, has obvious advantages that no other city in China can match. But almost every city in China does have a fast-growing population and residents who want to live in nicer homes. Moreover, many cities have taken a leaf out of Shanghai's technocratic playbook. Shanghai helped Pudong fill up by forcing banks to move there. Zhengzhou and Kunming, and to a lesser extent Ordos and Linyi, have followed suit by moving government offices, universities and schools. That means thousands of officials, students and teachers will populate new districts. And this is not a case of the government creating artificial demand: the number of university students in Zhengzhou and Kunming quadrupled between 2000 and 2010, so new campuses are needed. Zhengdong alone will accommodate 240,000 university students and teachers. The rationale is not only 'build it and they will come', but also 'build it and make them come'.

The experience of Dachang township on the northern edge of Shanghai suggests these tactics might work. Back in the late 1990s, when Shanghai University opened a US$160 million new campus there, the whitewashed buildings were marooned amid empty fields. The roads outside the campus were car-free, and students had nowhere to eat but the dreary student canteen. Getting into the city required waiting for an hourly bus, a ramshackle vehicle that listed severely to one side, belching black smoke from its exhaust pipe. The journey could take up to an hour and a half, but few students bothered, instead hunkering down to play endless games of cards.

Today the area around the university, once forlorn and desolate, has been transformed into a leafy and thriving suburb. The empty fields behind the campus are filled with restaurants, cafés, bars, noodle stalls and ice-cream parlours. There is a cinema and karaoke joint; gyms, book shops and internet cafés; a Walmart supermarket and a Suning household appliance store. The simple housing blocks built to accommodate dispossessed farmers are still there, but are now surrounded by smart compounds occupied by middle-class suburbanites. 'It's paradise these days,' says one returning ex-student, who recalls campus life ten years ago as a crushing bore.

The economic transformation is the result of several factors. The arrival of a critical mass of consumers created the conditions for private businesses to flourish, at the same time as rising property prices and population growth pushed more residents out of the city centre. Then, in 2009, the opening of a new metro line cut the commute into central Shanghai to just half an hour. The final factor in Dachang's transformation was less tangible but just as important: time. It took a decade for the old township to become the thriving suburb it is today.

The parallels with Zhengdong and Chenggong are obvious. Moving universities into a new area guarantees a critical mass of residents that encourages businesses to move with them. Like Shanghai University, the twenty-four universities setting up in Zhengdong and Chenggong will soon enjoy their own subway stations. And as these new areas develop, more residents from the old city are likely to move, too. So although these new districts look like a speculative leap of faith, local officials know they will not remain empty. If they can ensure the new districts have several hundred thousand residents, so the logic goes, the market will do the rest.

Given time, officials in Zhengzhou and Kunming will likely prove their doubters wrong. Zhengdong and Chengdong are attached to large provincial capitals and the basis for growth is obvious. That is less clear in Linyi, a much smaller city which may struggle to create enough jobs for an influx of people with few modern skills. The population pressure is real, however, and these new urbanites will have to be housed somewhere. China's urbanization process is riddled with inefficiency and waste. But new city districts and millions of empty apartments also reflect the size of the challenge facing a country that must build homes for hundreds of millions of people. China's 'ghost towns' are not as scary as they look.

Grey, ugly and congested: why are so many Chinese cities so horrible?

Ordos, Linyi, Zhengzhou and Kunming all have one thing in common: they are attempting to create new city districts with a pleasant living environment. This brings us to a conundrum that puzzles most outside visitors to China's cities. Even allowing for China's enormous population and still moderate level of economic development, why are so many Chinese cities so horrible? And why do they all look the same?

The typical Chinese city is grey, ugly and congested. It has pointlessly wide roads and squares, and functional, boxy buildings clad in grimy concrete or dirty white tiles. The old parts of town have been demolished, save perhaps for a solitary pagoda, rebuilt and sucked dry of its historical sap. The roads are jammed, the air filthy, the streets often unwalkable. Pavements and public entrances are blocked by private vehicles, whose owners scream abuse at cyclists and pedestrians for getting in their way. It is, in short, anything but 'liveable'.

China's leaders are not totally unaware of this depressing fact. In 2007 Qiu Baoxing, then vice minister of construction, launched a tirade against the dreary monotony of China's urban landscape.

He lambasted local officials for the 'senseless' destruction of the country's architectural and cultural heritage as China pursued its headlong rush towards modernization. Lamenting the ugly, uniform buildings casually erected on old temples and ancient streets, he put his finger on the most depressing aspect of modern Chinese urbanism. 'It is like having a thousand cities with the same appearance,' he complained.

China's vision of modernity is narrow, bloodless and disrespectful of the past. Government planners tear down old neighbourhoods in the name of 'development' and 'civilization'. Aside from a few exceptions, such as Beijing's dwindling ancient alleyways and Shanghai's colonial buildings, urban China has been almost entirely rebuilt since the 1950s. Most buildings today are less than thirty years old – typically square, six-storey apartment blocks made of bricks or cheap concrete. The few historical structures that have survived are invariably fenced off from the rest of the city and repackaged as an ersatz tourist experience. Often crudely reconstructed, they lose any evocative appeal they once held.

Even some of China's most celebrated cities are in danger of losing their soul. In Chengdu, locals wax lyrical about how their city is relaxed and liveable – but it is actually as grey, polluted, car-ridden and ugly as most other big Chinese cities. Many of its famous outdoor teahouses have moved into sterile shopping malls, and food stands are banished from the streets. Chongqing has done a better job of maintaining local character. Its side streets still buzz with stalls serving spicy noodles and other fiery local delicacies. After dusk, locals huddle around cauldrons of bubbling oil, fishing out slippery cubes of tofu and spicy jellies of pig's blood with glistening chopsticks. But Bo Xilai's attempts to 'civilize' Chongqing forced roadside hotpot joints out of the commercial district, and the city is noticeably less chaotic than it once was. Soon Chongqing's street life will be as dull as everywhere else.

Almost any Chinese official you meet can reel off a list of facts about his local city's magnificent history. In the same breath, he will tell you how many square metres of construction were completed in the previous year. Privately, many officials are fond of comparing their modernized cities favourably with the dilapidated slums they see in that other large and ancient Asian land – India. India's cities may be less modern than China's, but almost any Indian city you care to name has done a far better job of preserving its historical heritage. Indian cities, like those in Europe, possess the one element that so many of China's cities singularly lack: character.

城市化

China's urban landscape reflects its authoritarian system of government. During the Mao years, ancient cities were torn down and reconstructed on Soviet lines. The Soviet urban planning system used bold city master plans to create cities of inhuman scale: urban design was designed to project Communist Party power. In the 1950s, Beijing's city walls, a symbol of the hated feudal past, were demolished. The square in front of the Gate of Heavenly Peace – Tiananmen – was turned into the largest urban open space in the world. Historic courtyard homes were bulldozed to create avenues 100 metres wide. Similar destruction and rebuilding occurred in cities across China, albeit on a smaller scale.

China's cities continue to suffer from the legacy of Soviet-influenced urban planning, which focused on boosting industrial productivity and ensuring social control at the cost of all else. Local governments built vast new roads and public squares, compounds to house factories and workers, and universities to educate engineers and technicians. Cities were regarded as massive factories, or 'producer cities', rather than as social spaces. Function was everything; there was little interest in making cities pleasant places to live. This resulted in a uniformity of urban design that still shapes how cities look today.

The influence of Soviet design is one reason why Chinese cities look so alike. City planners still view Beijing as a model, whether consciously or not. The capital's power aesthetic is apparent in many new buildings across the country, especially those erected by local governments. Visit any Chinese city and you will find grandiose government buildings and expansive boulevards on the Beijing model. Some ordinary intersections in Chenggong, Kunming's new satellite city, are fully 200 metres wide. The central public square in Kangbashi, in Ordos, is nearly as large as Tiananmen Square. Buildings and cities across China are routinely built and laid out on a scale that is designed to shock and awe, not to produce a comfortable living environment.

Top-down planning does have its advantages. It ensures that houses are built, bridges constructed, subways dug. Hangzhou's master plan for 2001–20, for example, envisages moving all industry out of the city proper, building a 171-kilometre metro system, and expanding the airport to accommodate 30 million passengers. If officials say they will build something, they invariably do. 'The most striking difference between Chinese cities and cities almost anywhere else is that they build ahead to anticipate growth,' says Greg Clark, a London-based expert on city development who advises the municipal governments of some of the world's largest cities. 'In cities like São Paulo and Johannesburg, social and economic development is ahead of the physical infrastructure, which is constantly trying to catch up. In China it is the other way around.' By building infrastructure ahead of demand, Chinese planners are able to help direct the physical growth of the city. This is one reason why so many Chinese cities appear to have a surplus of housing and infrastructure, and also why fears about 'ghost towns' are so often overblown.

But top-down planning also has its limits. Long-term plans can fail to anticipate the messy reality of rapid development and may lock in planning errors. One example is Beijing's third ring road, which planners thought would serve as an efficient artery circling the core of the city. With few cars on the road in the early 1990s, planners followed the already outdated American practice of merging entrance and exit lanes. But as the number of private vehicles in

Beijing exploded from 1 million in 1997 to more than 5 million today, these ill-designed (not to mention dangerous) junctions became a major cause of congestion. Beijing's third ring road is consistently more jammed than other major arteries in the capital.

Long-term planning inevitably produces more uniformity than allowing cities to evolve organically. All municipal governments are required to produce a twenty-year master plan outlining general development goals, land-use patterns and a transport scheme. These are supposedly designed to address local needs, but one city's master plan often looks suspiciously like another's. Moreover, when city planners draw up designs for new districts, they must conform to certain national planning standards. The width of all new city roads, for example, must accord with regulations set in Beijing. The result is that dozens of new city districts all look the same.

Perhaps most damaging, China's cities often seem to be playthings for local officials rather than places for people to live. Power is concentrated in the hands of a few officials who are rewarded for boosting economic growth rather than providing public goods. Officials have a clear incentive to push for more development, however unneeded or badly planned, yet little incentive to listen to the concerns of residents. The result is unhealthy competition between cities, overinvestment and endless construction: more roads, new industrial parks, unnecessary airports, bigger government offices. Every city aspires to be a mini-Beijing, rather than catering to local needs.

This problem is exacerbated by China's system of government, which allows almost no public debate about how cities should develop. Residents are rarely consulted during the planning process for large development projects. Public monitoring only occurs once construction has started, or even after it has finished, by which time it is too late to turn back. 'The facts only emerge through disclosure by the mass media or public outcry,' says Xiaoyan Chen, a former urban planner at the China Academy of Urban Planning and Design. 'By then, negative social impact and economic loss are hard to alter' (Chen 2009: 7).

BOX 5.1 Kingdom of subways

What do almost all large, economically vibrant cities have in common? They have extensive public transport networks, usually with an efficient subway system. Exceptions are mostly found in the United States, with Los Angeles an obvious example. But Chinese cities do not have enough space to match the car ownership rates of the USA's energy-guzzling auto-cities. And even if they tried, the environmental impact would be too dire to imagine.

Chinese cities have no choice but to invest in mass rapid transit systems. Fortunately, if there is one thing China does well, it is infrastructure. China already has eighteen mass transit networks in operation (mainly subways, but also light rail and Shanghai's ultra-fast magnetic levitation train), with more than 2,000 kilometres of track. A further eighteen systems are under construction and due to open in 2012–17, while twenty-three more are at the planning stage. At 425 kilometres, Shanghai Metro has already overtaken the London Underground as the world's longest network. Beijing Subway, at 372 kilometres, ranks third ahead of New York City, but work is under way on lengthening the track to 1,000 kilometres by 2020.

These numbers are slightly misleading because most big cities in developed countries have additional commuter rail systems stretching out into the suburbs. A true accounting of New York's system would include the twenty or so commuter rail lines whose combined track far exceeds that of the subway system. As Chinese cities expand, they will have to spend more on above-ground commuter rail, which is the only effective way to bind together large urban areas. Moreover, the subway systems in Tokyo, Moscow and Seoul carry more passengers than those in Shanghai and Beijing.

Nevertheless, China's investment in subway systems is over-whelmingly positive. And there are also encouraging signs, too, that Chinese cities are beginning to shape urban development around public transport hubs. For example, Tiantongyuan, a high-density community of giant housing blocks in the suburbs of northern Beijing, has three subway stations. Shanghai's high-rise density has allowed it to retrofit its metro system as if it had always been there, and it has done a better job than Beijing of coordinating public transport with commercial development. 'Having learned from the experience of Hong Kong and Japanese cities, high-density development around [subway] stations is now widely accepted by local governments,' says Pan Haixiao, a professor of urban planning at Tongji University in Shanghai (Pan Haixiao 2011: 4). Still, no Chinese city has effectively copied Hong Kong's strategy of financing subway development by granting the right to build skyscrapers and shopping malls above its stations. MTR Corp, which runs Hong Kong's MTR metro system, is a listed company which made a profit of nearly US$2 billion in 2011.

Building efficient mass transit systems is a necessary step towards persuading urbanites to get out of their cars, or not to buy one in the first place. Even five years ago, wealthy urbanites would not have been seen dead on Beijing's subway – in stark contrast with cities such as London and New York, where hedge-fund managers (sometimes) rub shoulders with the proles. But attitudes have changed since the network expanded and the city government raised the cost of owning and using a car. Cars remain important status symbols, but experience shows that convenience can trump face.

This is important, because the greatest obstacle to reducing car usage in Chinese cities is changing people's mindset. In particular, public bicycle rental schemes must fight against a widely held view that cycling is a backward mode of transport that belongs in China's impoverished past. The proportion of people cycling to work in Beijing fell from nearly two-thirds in 1986 to just 18 per cent by 2010; yet 40 per cent of car journeys in the city were of less than 5 kilometres. In many cases cycling would be quicker and more convenient, but few businessmen want to be seen (or fear for their safety) on a bike.

One city where this attitude is changing is Hangzhou, where more than 60,000 bicycles are available for hire at 2,200 rental points around the city. The city government claims that the simple red bikes are used by more than 250,000 people per day, making it the biggest public bicycle rental service in the world. Cyclists swipe the bikes in and out with their city public transport card, which they must register under their state identification number. Renters pay nothing for the first hour, Rmb1 for the second hour, Rmb3 for three hours, and then a further Rmb3 for every extra hour – about 50 cents. The bikes, which feature advertising on their wheels and basket, have become so popular that Hangzhou is planning to increase their number to 90,000 by 2015.

Hangzhou's system is designed to facilitate short journeys and solve the 'last-mile' transport problem. Even the most sophisticated and best-funded public transport, after all, cannot deliver commuters to their front door. Bicycle rental schemes can supplement a well-designed public transport system, but not replace it. The key challenge for China's cities is to create mass public transport systems that connect seamlessly, making it more convenient to leave the car at home.

Local governments routinely spend grotesque sums on municipal vanity projects, often employing teams of international planners, architects and consultants. Competition with other cities means that if one city builds a swanky theatre or museum, theme park or Ferris wheel, other cities will want one too. Every major Chinese city today has its flashy, foreign-designed building – from Guangzhou's much-admired opera house to the striking new headquarters of China Central Television in Beijing. When smaller cities and districts turn to supposedly superior international planners the results can be positive – but they can also encourage grand designs and gimmicky projects that do more to fan officials' egos than serve local people.

Nonetheless, after half a century of soul-sapping utilitarianism, the pursuit of design is cheering in itself. The problem is that China's striking new buildings typically find themselves drowning in a sea of architectural dross. In a country that must house millions of new residents every year, cities and developers are under enormous pressure to build millions of apartments as quickly and cheaply as they can. City planners concentrate on nailing down a land-use plan, while developers roll out the same cookie-cutter apartments across the country. Aesthetic considerations are not high on the list of priorities, especially in a country where many people have become inured to unremitting ugliness.

As China becomes wealthier and people's standards begin to rise, urban design will improve. For the moment, however, most urban residents are far more concerned about price and comfort than aesthetics. The reality is that the urban landscape of a country that must house 1 billion people is never going to be beautiful.

城市化

A more pressing need than creating attractive cities is building cities that do not kill their inhabitants. The air pollution in urban China is horrific. Hundreds of cities are habitually shrouded in a brown or smoky fug that swallows buildings and bleaches the streets of colour. There is not much point in constructing signature buildings if no one can see them. Fewer than 20 per cent of China's cities meet World Health Organization standards for sulphur dioxide and nitrogen dioxide levels, and almost none for particulate matter. The air in dry, northern cities swirls with construction dust and sand blown off the Gobi Desert. China's cities emit 75 per cent of the country's greenhouse gases, and more than 400 are short of water.

As China's urban population expands to 1 billion, its cities will have to use resources more efficiently and enforce environmental regulations more rigorously. Cleaning up China's cities is more than a local concern: China is already the world's biggest greenhouse gas emitter, and emissions will continue to grow as the country urbanizes. China's economic model, which is reliant on heavy industry and manufacturing, means that energy usage is high for a country at China's level of development. In 2010, per-capita emissions were around six tons of carbon dioxide, equal with France. China's cities will struggle to improve air quality as long as car-ownership rates continue to soar and the country's power stations remain predominantly coal-fired. China may be the world's biggest producer of green technologies, but it still relies on coal for 70 per cent of its primary energy needs.

BOX 5.2 Beijing: Urban squires, city paupers

Wealthy Chinese urbanites traditionally lived in the city centre. In imperial Beijing they gathered in splendid courtyard houses set amid ancient alleyways shaded by scholar trees. Many wealthy Chinese today still choose to live centrally, although most prefer luxury apartments to dusty old courtyards. China has yet to experience the so-called 'doughnut' effect common in many US cities – a hollowing out of the inner city caused by moneyed professionals fleeing to the suburbs. Nevertheless, many Chinese cities are experiencing growing demand for a 'villa lifestyle': luxury detached homes set in quiet, leafy streets.

In both Beijing and Shanghai, many villas can be found on the way to the airport, conveniently located for ease of escape. Beijing's villa-land is centred on the old village of Tianzhu in the northeastern outskirts of the city. Here rural communities have been pushed out to make way for low-density, gated compounds – suburban retreats for rich locals and expats escaping the hustle and bustle of the city. The villa communities, each with its own club house and phalanx of beret-wearing guards, project a sense of exclusivity and unattainable luxury. The names – Merlin Champagne Town, Le Leman Lake, Yosemite Villas – proclaim their foreignness. Billboards outside one new development, built by the property arm of state food conglomerate COFCO Group, advertise entrance to the global elite: 'Paris time, New York time, Tokyo time. At Sky Villa they're all on Beijing time.'

One of the most luxurious villa compounds is Grasse Town, set on a tributary of the Wenyu River, 20 kilometres east of Beijing's central business district. Here bosses of state-owned enterprises and other well-connected sorts can snap up an 860-square-metre house, loosely styled on Californian mission architecture, for a cool US$9 million. The three-storey villas each boast a central courtyard, large garden, home cinema, bar and wine cellar. The best properties come with a view over a central lake, which is guarded by honking geese. Smaller, cheaper properties sell for a snip at just under US$3 million.

The gardens at Grasse Town are watered by the only river in Beijing that supposedly never runs dry. In 2006, the Beijing government spent US$200 million turning the banks of Wenyu River into an area of protected greenbelt or 'eco-corridor'. But in front of freshly planted trees, where signs instruct visitors to 'protect the local ecological environment', diggers tear up lush fields of grass to make way for a golf course. Both sides of the river are home to several golf courses, despite repeated promises by the central government to crack down on these illegal and, crucially, water-intensive developments.

This part of Beijing has become a playground of the rich. Pampered children learn to ride at the Tang Polo Club and slurp milkshakes in American-style diners. Yet the income disparities here are probably greater than anywhere else in the city. The International School of Beijing (ISB), which charges fees of US$30,000 per year, is backed by a migrant village with rubbish-strewn streets. Scantily clad children play in the gutter just a stone's throw from ISB's sumptuous facilities – a striking image of Beijing's extreme social stratification.

The central government is trying hard to lower the amount of energy it uses to produce each unit of GDP growth. 'In China you can go to any city, big or small, and they will have energy efficiency targets to meet. I have not seen that anywhere else in the world,' says Ede Ijjasz, head of the China and Mongolia Sustainable Development Unit at the World Bank. Almost 200 Chinese cities have low-carbon or 'eco-city' targets. But at the city level there is often far more talk than action. The vast majority of so-called 'eco-cities' are anything but ecologically sound. For many local governments and developers, describing a city or building as 'green' is little more than a useful branding tool. Even those cities that invest in low-carbon construction or fancy waste disposal schemes tend to have wide roads and free parking. Rather than wasting money on a handful of expensive and dubious eco-cities, China would do much better to ensure that all new buildings are properly insulated.

Chinese cities have done a better job of mobilizing human resources to improve the environment, planting millions of trees and
shrubs to help filter dust particles and freshen the air. Official
statistics state that the total area of 'green land' in China's cities
grew from 475,000 hectares in 1990 to more than 2 million hectares
in 2010. Changing city boundaries and a liberal definition of what
constitutes 'green land' mean these numbers should be taken with
a pinch of salt: few residents would believe the official claim that
nearly 40 per cent of the area of Chinese cities is green. Moreover,
many environmentalists doubt the effectiveness of planting mono-
cultures of new trees, few of which are ever allowed to grow to
their full height. Still, many urbanites have seen decrepit housing
demolished to make way for new parks, and Chinese cities are
noticeably less grey than they were a decade ago.

Greening cities is important, but amounts to tinkering at the
edges. The most practical way for China to create more liveable,
sustainable cities would be to enforce restrictions on car usage, crack
down on urban sprawl, and invest in mass rapid transit systems.
Dense, compact cities served by public transport are far more energy
efficient than cities with sprawling, car-dependent suburbs. The
good news is that Chinese cities are investing heavily in new subway
networks. The bad news is that cities are rapidly expanding and
suburbanizing, thanks to demand for more living space and exploding car ownership. This matters because the shape of cities built
today will help determine energy demand and influence consumer
behaviour for many years to come.

Beijing, with its car-dependent economy and five ring roads, is
a fine example of how to create a city that is not environmentally
sustainable. Few cities have expanded more noticeably than the
capital, whose city districts today are six times larger than they were
in the 1970s. In the 1990s, the municipal government designated
car manufacturing a pillar industry but, unlike Shanghai, failed to
restrict car ownership. As the city expanded and car ownership rose,
planners shaped urban land use around an expanding road network.

The construction of each new ring road encouraged the city to sprawl, while the radial expansion put more and more pressure on commuter arteries into the city centre. Twenty years on, the results are plain to see: Beijing suffers from appalling congestion and air pollution; the city is spread out, with a lower population density than other large Chinese cities; and residents suffer some of the longest commutes anywhere in the world.

One of the most pressing problems in a city of high-rises is finding enough space to park. New housing developments must have underground parking – but Beijing's older neighbourhoods were not designed to accommodate hundreds of vehicles. Pavements are crammed with cars, and double parking is standard on many streets. Many of the city's children have nowhere to play outside: all available public space is occupied by vehicles. The problem is far more serious in Beijing than in the USA or Western Europe, and is set to spread to many other cities across the country. Once a positive sign of growing wealth, the capital's car boom is now undoubtedly lowering the quality of life.

As China's urban residents grow richer, they will begin to demand cleaner air and a more pleasant living environment. In wealthy cities such as Shanghai, Hangzhou and, for all its faults, Beijing, this process is well under way. If Chinese cities want to be globally and nationally competitive, they cannot rely on economic growth alone to attract and retain talented, creative residents. If China's urban dream is to remain intact, city planners and officials must work harder to create healthy cities in which people want to live. That means cleaning up the filthy air, investing in public transport, restricting urban sprawl, and respecting cultural heritage. It also means learning when too much planning can stifle a city's soul.

BOX 5.3 Hangzhou: preservation with Chinese characteristics

Since it became the magnificent capital of the Southern Song dynasty more than 800 years ago, Hangzhou has been prized for its beauty. Countless poets have been inspired by the view over the famous West Lake, whose misty waters are lined with swaying willow trees, ornamental bridges and ancient temples. But for the city authorities today, this means one thing: tourist dollars.

A decade ago, Chinese tourists were easy to satisfy: all they wanted was a photo of themselves standing next to a famous 'scenic spot', preferably one ranked high on the government's list of tourist attractions. All important scenic and tourist spots in China are given an official rating, following the (unofficial) Chinese rule that any object, idea or place must be properly quantified and categorized. Not only is Hangzhou's West Lake a national 5A tourist resort – the top ranking available – it is even a Unesco World Heritage Site. This is a double whammy that few other Chinese cities can boast.

All this means that Hangzhou is not short of visitors. But Chinese tourists are becoming more demanding. As they grow richer and better travelled, they want more than a photo and a bag of local snacks. Increasingly, they also demand shops, bars, teahouses and restaurants, preferably selling characteristic local produce served up in a 'traditional' setting. The experience of visiting a place is gradually becoming as important as the act of visiting itself, even if that experience is more tourist tat than truly authentic.

The Hangzhou government has cottoned on to this change of mindset and is doing what it can to deliver an experience of the 'old' city. The focus has been on reconstructing and renovating the ancient streets and buildings that fan east of the old (reconstructed) drum tower. A decade ago, Hefang and Zhongshan streets maintained some of their traditional charm, lined with dilapidated courtyard houses with traditional whitewashed walls and grey-tiled roofs, or featuring handsome Western architecture from the Republican period of the early twentieth century. But the streets were also run-down, snarled with cars, and blighted with ugly modern buildings.

In 2004, the city government launched a 'comprehensive protection and organic reconstruction project'. Government archaeologists dug up the road to reveal layers of paving stone dating to the Southern Song, Yuan, Ming and Qing dynasties. The reconstruction focused on trying to re-create the feel of the old town, including restoring an ancient waterway, long since buried under new stone and asphalt. Few genuinely old buildings have survived, and many have been built from scratch in 'traditional' style. Buildings with original, restored exteriors have been gutted, retrofitted and turned into modern shops. The result is commercial, but largely tasteful and pleasant.

Today locals and tourists saunter down pedestrianized streets lined with flowing streams. Some fine old buildings have been restored to their former glory, including the famous Zhongdetang traditional Chinese medicine shop, built around a magnificent courtyard, which dates back to 1808. Hypochondriacs crowd to the old dispensary to buy mysterious packets of dried fungus carefully stored in shiny wooden drawers. Many Western-style buildings, too, have been scrubbed up and could sit comfortably on the riverside Bund at the heart of the Shanghai's old International Settlement, even if they do house McDonald's or Häagen-Dazs.

Hangzhou took its lead from Shanghai, whose wildly successful renovation of a block of traditional 'stone-gate' houses showed the city government that restoring old buildings could be more lucrative than demolishing them. Snooty foreigners often complain that Xintiandi, as the shopping and restaurant complex is called, is *faux* traditional – a Disneyfied version of Old Shanghai. But the precedent set by Shanghai is an important one in a country where, until recently, few people valued the architectural fabric of their past.

The idea of restoring charming but decrepit old neighbourhoods is now being copied by several other cities in China. The onus is typically on reconstruction, which means demolishing and rebuilding, rather than genuine restoration. Beijing's redevelopment of the Qianmen area south of Tiananmen Square is a case in point, although the reconstructed streets here are a considerable improvement on the choked and tatty thoroughfares they had become. But the southwest city of Kunming is doing a more sensitive job of restoring a block of wooden, shuttered houses and ancient courtyards in the city centre. These two-storey buildings used to house the city's bustling bird and flower market, but many have clumps of grass growing out of their tiled roofs and are on the verge of falling down. The local authorities hope the area will become the city's own Xintiandi, which literally translates as 'New Heaven on Earth'.

Complaints that local reconstruction projects risk destroying some of the few remnants of the past that survive in China's relentlessly modern cities contain more than a sliver of truth. Without them, however, the buildings would probably be torn down in any case. As more tourists demand a 'traditional' experience in China's cities, reconstruction efforts may shift towards genuine restoration and preservation. Any attempt to respect cultural heritage and preserve local urban character should be applauded.

BOX 5.4 Tianjin: scrubbing up

Exiting Tianjin station used to be a dispiriting experience – like arriving in grimy Middlesbrough in northeast England or rundown Bridgeport in Connecticut, only worse. But thanks to a major city redevelopment scheme, all that has changed. The honking three-wheel taxis and hotel touts that used to assault visitors have disappeared. Instead, a giant piazza leads down to a riverside boardwalk lined with landscaped gardens and colonial architecture. Whisper it, but China's fourth city is almost *nice*.

Tianjin's history as a treaty port, in which successive European powers and Japan built self-contained concessions, always gave it tourist potential. But until the late 2000s, the city's fine colonial buildings lay neglected as it tried to forget its humiliating past. Tianjin remained famous across China for its local steamed buns, sweet twisted dough sticks and stand-up comedians. But few people wanted to visit this large, grimy, polluted city.

The transformation over the past few years has been remarkable. The focus is the Hai River, which runs through the centre of the city. The city government has renovated the fine array of Western buildings on the riverbank and replaced ugly brutalist architecture with replicas of old colonial mansions. Now tourists in open riverboats glide past the handsome new-old buildings, whose burgundy-tiled roofs glisten in the sun. Passengers disgorging from the railway station can walk across the handsome iron-rivet Liberation Bridge, constructed in 1927, to the gleaming new World Financial Centre. At 337 metres, it is taller than any building in Europe.

Further down the river, crowds lunch al fresco in the restored former Italian Concession, sitting at tables in cobbled squares. Meanwhile, fans of British colonial architecture can step back 150 years in the newly restored Astor Hotel, where former US president Herbert Hoover was a regular visitor during his days as a mining engineer in China. Most tourists from the capital return on the high-speed shuttle service, which leaves every ten minutes and completes the 115-kilometre journey in half an hour.

Just a decade ago, Tianjin was a quintessential modern Chinese city: big, ugly, charmless. Most of the city is still unattractive, but the Tianjin government deserves enormous credit for stopping the rot, restoring the long-neglected colonial quarters, and turning the city into a viable tourist destination. Some things, however, have yet to change. Outside the futuristic new St Regis hotel on the riverside walkway, a short stroll from the World Financial Centre, two old men unzip their flies and urinate casually on the pavement. Tianjin has scrubbed up, but it retains the rough edge of old.

BOX 5.5 Zhengzhou: the beauty in the beast

In Zhengzhou's Erqi Square, at the centre of the shopping district, construction workers in yellow hard hats are building the city's first subway system. They scurry in and out of a giant hole in the road, criss-crossed with concrete bars and steel poles. The first line will open in 2013 or 2014, and is sorely needed. The resident population in the city is approaching 6 million; a further 5 million people live in the surrounding countryside and satellite towns. Like every other sizeable Chinese city, Zhengzhou's roads are gridlocked and its air polluted. 'Every day there are terrible traffic jams, and we never see a blue sky,' moans Sun Weibin, a retired soldier who has lived in the city for much of his life.

At first glance, there is little to recommend Zhengzhou. Henan's capital is a gritty, chaotic and congested place, unlovely even by the standards of so many Chinese cities. It creaks under the strain of people, cars and dangerous swarms of electronic bikes, which whoosh silently past on the pavement. But, like many Chinese cities, there is more to Zhengzhou than meets the eye. Veer off the bustling high street and the pace of life slows: old ladies sit on the street playing cards and men chat, shirtless in the late afternoon heat. The street is lined with vegetable stalls, repair shops and dingy, hole-in-the-wall restaurants. The area is poor, but it has a vitality and neighbourliness that cannot be found in the identikit apartment blocks sprouting all over the city.

On summer nights, when locals emerge onto the streets after their evening meal, Zhengzhou even gains a ragged charm. Ignoring the perennially smog-clotted air, citizens – young and old – stroll along the banks of the Golden River. In reality, this is a murky, concrete-lined cesspool. But in China reality doesn't matter very much – it's the idea that counts. Housewives stop for an open-air back rub on makeshift stretcher-beds set up by amateur masseurs. Children jump on bouncy castles and toss shiny, luminous rings into the air. Giggling lovers walk hand in hand, whispering in dark corners. And retired folk gather in the park to belt out the revolutionary songs of their youth, singing the praises of the long-dead Chairman Mao.

First impressions in Zhengzhou, then, are misleading. Take Driver Wang, a local taxi driver with a breezeblock head, and one of the toughest-looking men you are ever likely to meet. His forearms, darkly bronzed like the silt-laden earth of the Yellow River plain and covered with home-scratched tattoos, are as thick as a maturing sapling. Stubby, powerful fingers are attached to visibly muscled hands that could easily crush a child's skull. The underside of his chin is roughly scarred, as if someone once tried to cut his throat. But Wang possesses a sweet-natured smile, and on closer inspection his tattoos spell out a traditional Confucian saying. 'Honour one's parents', the crude strokes instruct. Like Zhengzhou itself, Wang is tough and unpretty, but ultimately good-natured.

6

A Billion Wallets: What China's
New Urbanites Will and Won't Buy

The immense flatlands of the North China Plain are dry, dusty and uninviting. In winter, the endless fields turn a dispiriting grey-brown, denuded of colour and vitality. Electricity pylons march across a featureless landscape punctuated by compact villages arranged in practical, collective squares. This may seem an unlikely region to understand China's urban consumption. In fact, it is the perfect place to start.

One typical village is Dazhangshan. Located at the southern edge of Hebei province, not far from the borders with Henan and Shandong, Dazhangshan can be reached in three hours from Beijing along an empty expressway. The village's 2,000 residents, almost all of whom are cotton farmers, live in brick courtyard homes running off a single main road, which was concreted for the first time in 2008. During the spring planting season, when powerful winds blow across the plain and whip topsoil off the freshly ploughed fields, villagers cover their heads with towels in a vain effort to keep out the grit. From November to March, when agricultural work grinds to a halt, they huddle at home, play mah-jong, and do their best to keep warm.

Traditionally, China's hundreds of millions of farmers lived a subsistence lifestyle. They ate what they grew, and had no income to spend. But over the past decade or so, that began to change. In the 1990s, under the leadership of President Jiang Zemin and Premier Zhu Rongji, government policies focused almost exclusively on China's cities. Urban incomes grew rapidly and the gap with the countryside widened. But their successors, Hu Jintao and Wen Jiabao, did a better job of rural policy. Under their leadership, China abolished its age-old rural land taxes and expanded the social safety net into rural areas. As rural incomes rose, hundreds of millions of rural households were able to buy their first television, washing machine and refrigerator. This raised the prospect that China's huge rural populace, which is as large as the populations of the United States and Western Europe combined, could become a massive consumer market in its own right. A number of reports even claimed that the rural consumer had arrived.

Visiting Dazhangshan, where annual household incomes and expenditure match the national rural average, shows why any excitement about the rural consumer is nonsense. Certainly farmers' lives have improved dramatically in recent years, and rural households no longer live an entirely subsistence existence. But villagers are far from becoming the modern consumers dreamed about by marketing executives in Shanghai, let alone in New York or Tokyo. They have neither the incomes nor the opportunity. Urban household consumption growth stubbornly continues to outpace rural consumption, and urbanites spend nearly four times more than their rural cousins. In 2010, rural residents spent just US$600 each; half of this went on subsistence purchases of food and clothing. The reality is that rural incomes – and hence rural consumption levels – remain extremely low.

Dazhangshan's spring fair, which turns the village into a bustling marketplace, provides a useful gauge of local attitudes to consumption. As farmers take a break from the fields and children get the day off school, local entrepreneurs set up makeshift stalls selling food, toys, clothes and household goods. At the small village temple – dedicated to Guanyin, the Buddhist goddess of mercy – older villagers light incense, kowtow before the shrine, and chant above a cacophony of clanging symbols. Younger villagers walk the bustling streets and check out the deals on offer. One roadside market doing a brisk trade offers all goods for just a few cents: plastic mugs, children's books, knives, plugs, screwdrivers, tin saucepans. Other stalls sell shirts, sweaters and shoes for a few dollars each, while fruit sellers offer a rare treat of strawberries, bananas and pineapples. Children lick ice creams and pester their parents to buy flimsy plastic toys.

This is as far as casual consumerism goes in a Chinese village. Once the stalls are packed away and life returns to normal, daily consumption is minimal. Villagers say they are beginning to spend more than they used to, mainly on food and drink. But most meals are still prepared from scratch using home-grown ingredients. Typically, breakfast and dinner are a simple porridge made of millet, perhaps with fried vegetables or buns of steamed bread. Lunch, the main meal of the day, might be pork and noodles, served in a rich, meaty broth. 'Back in the 1960s, we didn't have enough money to buy meat at Spring Festival,' says Li Hongqi, a cotton farmer with a handsome, weather-beaten face. 'But now we eat meat nearly every day!' He grins and downs a full glass of *baijiu*, China's fiery grain spirit. In the winter, villagers enjoy fresh vegetables imported from south China, in addition to the monotonous traditional diet of pickled cabbage.

One of Dazhangshan's two stores sells simple household items: thermos flasks, plastic bowls, shampoo, towels. The other offers cheap packaged food and drinks, such as processed sausages, sweets, milk powder and bottles of *baijiu*. In the evening, the shop doubles as a restaurant, where a meal washed down with a bottle of watery local beer costs about US$1.50. On the street outside, local traders sell fresh vegetables from the back of their minivans and village pig-breeders hang pork cuts from metal hooks. Most families in Dazhangshan own a cheap mobile phone, and China

Mobile maintains a service centre in the village. But there is little else to buy in the village, and the windswept county town of Nangong, 15 kilometres away, is hard to get to. Few households own a road vehicle, and most rarely leave the village.

Li's sparsely furnished home shows just how far an average rural family is from becoming an urban-style consumer. The house is built around a high-walled courtyard to keep out the dusty spring winds; the floors are made of rough brick and the walls smoothed with tamped earth. 'Cement is better because it doesn't flake and fall off, but you have to pay for it,' he explains. An old television flickers in the corner, and the main room is lit by single fluorescent light tube. The furniture consists of a small wooden table and two chairs, an old sofa, a wardrobe, and a flimsy foldable table with stools. The only decoration is a free supermarket calendar showing images of Chinese fighter jets. Like all the houses in the village, water is collected from a tap in the yard. The lavatory is an earthen pit outside, hidden behind a wall.

China's central government has come up with a number of schemes to boost rural consumption. In 2008, policymakers introduced a 13 per cent subsidy on household appliances in rural areas, hoping that rural families would fill their homes with shiny DVD players, fridges and air-conditioners. Every household in Dazhangshan was able to buy three subsidized items by showing their red *hukou* book at designated markets in nearby towns. Yet few villagers took advantage of the subsidies, which ended in 2011, despite government claims that the scheme was a massive success. 'We already have a television and a washer, and we only replace things when they break,' says Li's brother, reflecting a common sentiment. Only around half of all households in Dazhangshan and neighbouring villages own a fridge, while air-conditioning is a luxury few can afford. 'If farmers don't need something, they won't buy it,' says a shop assistant selling air-conditioners in Nangong.

Most farmers will only consume when there is a good economic reason to do so. In 2009, policymakers came up with a second round of subsidies, this time lowering the sales tax rate on small, cheap vehicles. Before the scheme kicked in, there were almost no non-farm vehicles in Dazhangshan. But by spring 2010, the village had eight Hafei minivans, each costing around US$6,000; two second-hand sedans, including an old Volkswagen Santana; and a new Xiali, a cheap domestic brand of car. Minivans and cars are the tools of trade for petty rural businessmen hoping to escape the drudgery of the fields. Most of the locals from surrounding villages who came to celebrate Dazhangshan's spring fair that year arrived on bicycles and motorbikes. But a sprinkling of friends and relatives drove cheap Chinese-brand vehicles – including BYDs, whose name supposedly stands for 'Build Your Dreams'. Motorcycles and tractors remain by far the most common form of motorized transport in the village, but the rural market for low-cost cars and minivans is gathering momentum.

Dazhangshan, like the vast majority of Chinese villages, remains poor. As incomes rise, villagers are eating better, improving their living conditions, and leading more comfortable lives. The sheer size of China's rural population means that small increases in individual household consumption look impressive in the aggregate. And for makers of inexpensive cars, household appliances and cheap household goods – particularly makers of packaged foods and basic toiletries, such as Procter & Gamble and Unilever – the rural market is no longer a black hole. But rising household spending does not mean that China's 650 million or so rural residents are about to become genuine consumers. Consumption is far from the level needed to excite many big domestic brands, not to mention foreign retailers waiting for the next big market to take off.

For all the talk of China's growing rural market, rural incomes are not high enough to drive national consumption. Moreover, the shrinking size of the rural population means that rural consumers will actually become less important as a proportion of the national market over time. Most of the increase in Chinese consumption over the next decade will come from urban areas, not from China's

700,000 villages. In China's cities, income levels are higher and there are many more opportunities to spend. Hundreds of millions of rural people will become consumers over the coming decades – but only when they leave the farm and start to lead urban lives. For consumption to become a genuine engine of economic growth, China must look to its cities.

城市化

Foreign businessmen have salivated over the enormous potential of the Chinese consumer for more than two hundred years. In the nineteenth century, British merchants used to say that 'just adding an inch to every Chinaman's shirt tail will keep Manchester's cotton industry going for ever'. When the Chinese court refused to open its market to foreign goods and banned imports of Indian opium, Britain responded with force.

Today, China is awash with foreign-made goods and domestic products alike. Its retail markets are booming. But critics of China's economic model argue that consumption plays too small a role in driving economic growth. They argue that China's economy is far too reliant on building things, and its people spend too little. Investment's share of GDP shot up from 35 per cent in 2000 to 49 per cent in 2010, while household consumption's share shrank from an already measly 46 per cent to just 34 per cent. No other country has ever grown with such a high share of investment and such a low level of consumption – not even South Korea, whose experience of economic take-off most resembles China's. China's investment-driven model of economic development is widely viewed as both wasteful and unsustainable.

This is not only a domestic problem. Some analysts accuse China's economic model, which relies on artificially keeping interest rates at rock-bottom levels, of stoking global imbalances. Cheap credit keeps China's industrial machine whirring, but low deposit rates discourage households from consuming. For much of the past decade, real deposit rates were negative: households earned less on their savings than the rate of inflation. At home, this meant that families put aside more cash to pay for education, health care and retirement, leaving less cash for casual consumption. But the effects of China's savings glut were felt elsewhere – notably in the United States and parts of Europe, where consumers plugged China's consumption deficit by consuming far more than they had the money to pay for. According to this view, China deserves its share of blame for fuelling the global recession.

The argument that financial repression in China played a major role in stoking the global financial crisis is contentious. But few analysts, least of all China's own policymakers, disagree that the economy needs to 'rebalance'. In March 2012, at the annual meeting of China's parliament, Premier Wen Jiabao told delegates that China's investment-heavy growth pattern was 'unbalanced, uncoordinated and unsustainable'.

Urbanization is clearly part of the solution to putting China's economy on a more even keel. Even the poorest migrant workers earn far more than the average farmer, which should mean they can afford to spend more. And life in the city not only encourages, but also requires, far more absolute consumption than life in the village. Urbanites must pay for food, water, electricity and transport, and city living provides many more opportunities to buy goods and services. By contrast, few villages have many (if any) shops, and the nearest county town may be an hour's drive away along rutted farm tracks. From an environmental perspective, turning millions of farmers into urban consumers sounds like a nightmare in the offing. But from an economic viewpoint, China needs to shift the onus of economic growth towards greater domestic demand. One notable advocate for the economic merits of faster urbanization is the incoming premier, Li Keqiang. Cleaning up the mess, China's leaders believe, can come later.

Economically, there is much that is valid in this argument, yet urbanization should not be viewed as a magic cure for all ills. In the first place, the process of moving more people off the farm will not immediately correct the imbalance between investment and consumption. The reason is that urban households save much more, and consume a much lower proportion of their income, than subsistence farmers. As more rural households move to the city, consumption will rise quickly – but so, too, will savings. And because China's banking system is largely set up to funnel savings into industrial investment, this means the ratio of consumption as a share of national income is unlikely to rise substantially. It may even fall. This, in fact, is precisely what happened over the past decade.

More investment is not necessarily a bad thing. In rapidly urbanizing countries, household savings need to be channelled into building more apartments, roads and bridges. Huge investment in cities is the flipside of mass migration; without it, China's cities would collapse and the urbanization process would fail. As long as urbanization remains rapid, therefore, the role of investment in China's economy should remain strong. This means that any rebalancing of China's domestic economy over the next ten or fifteen years will happen only slowly. The idea that China can shift overnight to a consumption-led economy is pure fantasy.

In the second place – and most importantly – the expansion of the urban population will not instantly create a new middle class of consumers. The bulk of China's urban population growth will come from low-income rural migrants with little money to spend and almost no experience of personal consumption. Simply moving a farmer into a flat does not make him an economically significant consumer. On the contrary, if policymakers do not extend social welfare to migrants and fail to integrate them into the urban economy, greater urbanization could merely create a gargantuan urban underclass.

To boost urban consumption, therefore, China's government needs to take action on three fronts. First, it must allow rural migrants to become full urban citizens. Second, it must pursue policies that help to raise household incomes. And third, it must reduce incentives for high saving by urban households. The last has two components:

providing a stronger social safety net, and increasing the financial returns for household savers, so that households have more money left over to consume. Only by creating a more socially inclusive form of urbanization and by putting more money in people's pockets will China learn to consume more than it invests.

Encouragingly, there are growing signs that China's leaders agree with this analysis. More than fifty years after it was introduced, cautious moves are afoot to reform the *hukou* system and speed up rural-to-urban migration. And clearer land rights are enabling a growing number of farmers to rent out their land. These changes are piecemeal, and the most ambitious plans are still limited to two pilot projects in Chengdu and Chongqing. But provincial and city governments nationwide keenly pursue urbanization targets, and more policymakers are banging the drum for speedier urbanization. Liu He, an economic advisor to Hu Jintao, estimates that each percentage point increase in the urbanization rate adds 0.4 points to GDP growth.

So far, however, China has patently failed to capture the full economic potential of moving hundreds of millions of people off the farm. Certainly the productivity gains have been enormous: in the ugly jargon beloved by economists, migrants add far more 'value' when they are moulding plastic or mopping city floors than they do planting crops. But the majority of these new factory and service workers have not become real consumers. Migrant households typically earn about US$3,000–8,000 per year, not enough to leave much spare cash for shopping. More than 70 per cent of migrant households currently spend US$80–320 per month, of which half goes on food. The typical migrant family earns two-thirds of the urban average, placing them in the bottom 20 per cent of urban earners.

Migrant households' real disposable income is even lower than the income data suggest, because so few migrant workers receive urban social security. With little or no financial protection against illness or unemployment, they squirrel away 50 per cent of their earnings. Although the household registration system is not quite as socially divisive as it once was, the lack of a local *hukou* still means that the vast majority of migrants cannot live as full urban citizens. Most migrant workers lead self-contained lives isolated from ordinary urban society. They may live in the city, but they continue to consume like rural residents – barely at all. This phenomenon, which critics have dubbed 'incomplete urbanization', means that one-third of China's urban residents are effectively shut out of the urban consumer economy. So long as migrants do not receive pensions or adequate health insurance, subsidized housing or education for their children, they will save rather than spend.

A more inclusive form of urbanization, on the other hand, could unleash a wave of demand – not only for consumer goods, but also for urban infrastructure and housing. 'Urban construction currently does not take migrants' demand for public infrastructure into account, and migrants themselves do not consume like urban locals,' says Cai Fang, director of the Institute of Population and Labour Economics at the China Academy of Social Sciences (CASS). 'Therefore, both individual and public consumption, which could have resources to spur economic growth especially in the service sector, has been depressed. Only by abolishing the *hukou* system and making migrants legal city citizens can we make the most of urbanization as the engine of economic growth' (Cai 2010: 86). A 2011 survey by the Ministry of Housing and Urban–Rural Development found that a 50 per cent increase in migrant workers' paltry spending on non-food and housing items would boost retail sales by two percentage points.

If rural migrants became full urban citizens, there is good reason to believe their consumption would take off. The younger generation of migrants born in the 1980s and 1990s are far more likely to consume than the older generation. They are better educated and many see their future in the city. Migrants may earn less than other urbanites, Cai contends, but they also have a stronger marginal propensity to consume than urban natives. Experience from other emerging markets in Asia, as well as data from China's own spending habits, shows that consumption levels increase significantly once annual disposable income hits around US$10,000 per household. If incomes rose by around one-third, many migrant households would cross this threshold.

Cheeringly, the process of putting more money in migrants' pockets has already begun, even without substantial progress in *hukou* reform. For most of the past twenty years, migrant wage growth did not keep up with the overall economy, and the almost endless supply of young migrants entering the workforce allowed employers to squeeze them dry. But demographic changes mean that situation is set to reverse: economists at CASS predict that growth in the number of workers entering the labour force will fall to zero by 2015, and then shrink. The total supply of young workers entering the labour force will drop by roughly one-third in the period 2010–22, which should require businesses to pay more for entry-level workers. In theory, this wage pressure will percolate through the entire migrant labour force, driving up migrants' wages and therefore their ability to consume.

Rapidly rising minimum wages in dozens of cities across China are evidence that China's labour market has already begun to tighten. This means that migrant labourers will increasingly be able to vote with their feet, forcing employees to provide them with better working conditions. Encouragingly, a report published in 2011 by the China Labour Bulletin (CLB), a Hong Kong-based NGO, argued persuasively that migrant workers are indeed gaining more leverage over their employers. The report catalogued dozens of cases that show how a more organized labour movement and collective wage negotiations have pushed up labour costs since 2009.

The two most high profile examples came in Guangdong, southern China's manufacturing heartland, in 2010. When Taiwanese electronics company Foxconn was hit by a spate of suicides at its mammoth Shenzhen plant, hostile media accused Foxconn of mistreating its workers. This was probably somewhat unfair: Foxconn runs a disciplined ship, and conditions in its factories are far better than in thousands of smaller workshops run by cowboy businessmen. Nevertheless, the combination of employee unrest and critical reporting forced Foxconn to double basic wages in Shenzhen to more than US$320 for production-line workers. The protests at Foxconn were followed by debilitating strikes at Honda's automotive components factory in Foshan, a factory city on the edge of Guangzhou. Honda responded with pay increases in excess of 25 per cent.

CLB's report concluded: 'The government and employers have been put on notice that the standard business model of the last two decades, of management dictating pay and working conditions to their employees, is no longer sustainable' (China Labour Bulletin 2011: 12). Wage data support this finding, showing that real wages have risen across the board. The most useful proxy for migrant wages – the wage component in the rural household survey – grew by around 15 per cent after inflation in 2011. This included non-agricultural wages earned by farmers in the countryside, but largely reflected wages paid to migrants working in factories or on construction sites. Crucially, government policies are reinforcing rather than blocking this shift. Almost every province or municipality raised minimum wages in 2010, by an average of 23 per cent. In 2011, big employers of migrant labour such as Beijing and Guangzhou raised minimum wages again, signalling a move towards annual wage adjustments. In early 2012, following yet more adverse media coverage, Foxconn raised wages for its 1.2 million Chinese workers by a further 16–25 per cent.

The Chinese government may not enjoy the social instability of industrial action, but it does not seem opposed to efforts by factory workers to secure higher wages. In May 2010, the Ministry of Human Resources and Social Security issued a circular stating that collective contract systems should be introduced at all enterprises with established trade unions by the end of 2012. These moves recognize the reality that the 'new generation' of migrant workers born after 1980 are now the mainstream of the workforce. They are better educated than the first generation, less tolerant of poor pay and conditions, and more inclined to collective action. Collective bargaining almost guarantees wage increases in excess of the minimum wage, which in any case tends to lag behind market wages. Higher wages for migrant workers are in line with the government policy to boost household incomes and create a fairer society.

China's changing demographics mean that wages in China's factories should continue to rise. That is good news for the 90 million or so migrant workers currently employed in manufacturing. But most of the new jobs that China must create over the next twenty years will come from services, not manufacturing. Global demand for consumer goods has slowed significantly since the global financial crisis, and rising labour costs mean that some low-end production will inevitably move to other countries. Boosting services' share of GDP – which stood at a paltry 43 per cent in 2011, compared to 58 per cent in South Korea and 75 per cent in Japan – is a long-term government policy. China's leaders know that the urbanization process will not succeed, ultimately, unless new urbanites find work and fully participate in urban life.

This is where the danger of forcing farmers with few urban skills into cities looms large. Faster urbanization has the potential to create hundreds of millions of new urban consumers, but it is also a potential recipe for mass urban poverty. Urbanization will only work if farmers can create a viable life for themselves in the city. If the economy does not create enough jobs, China could easily find itself succumbing to the same bleak predicament as many Western societies: handing over welfare payments to a disenfranchised urban underclass living in run-down public housing estates.

城市化

The potential of China's urban consumer economy is huge, yet without the right policies it could easily continue to disappoint. Reports on the Chinese consumer tend to swing between two extremes: hysterical excitement provoked by the idea of a billion open wallets, and endless gloom about the continued failure of consumption to take over as the engine of economic growth.

If you believe the most excitable reports, France's economy would sink into the English Channel were it not for the throngs of Chinese shoppers eagerly snapping up the latest trinkets from Louis Vuitton and Chanel. If you prefer the doom-laden wittering of the much-quoted 'China bears' – sceptical international investors who believe that China is a gigantic bubble waiting to burst – the nation's households are actually so squeezed by financial repression that they hardly have any money left with which to shop. The truth is somewhere in between.

Certainly visitors to big, rich cities like Shanghai and Beijing have long questioned all the fuss about weak Chinese consumption. Casual consumption, especially among the under-forties, is everywhere. Even ten years ago, Chinese magazines were regaling their readers with tales of *yueguangzu*, 20-something wage splurgers in big cities who spent their entire monthly salary before the next payday. But these conspicuous consumers were until recently a tiny minority of the population. GK Dragonomics estimates that in 2005 only 40 million households (120 million people) belonged to what it terms 'Consuming China', with an average yearly expenditure of US$5,000. That left 90 per cent of the population in the 'Surviving China' camp, consisting of well over 1 billion people operating at a subsistence level or just above.

This distinction still holds, but the size of Consuming China has grown enormously. In 2009, China had an America-sized population of 100 million households (300 million people) with annual expenditures of around US$7,500, nearly one-quarter of the population. Another estimate by the Boston Consulting Group (BCG) in 2010 used a slightly higher threshold to define the household wealth of 'middle income and affluent consumers', but came up with similar findings. It found that 50 million households, about 150 million people, had an annual disposable income of US$9,000 or more, at 2005 prices. And these findings relied on official household survey data, which many economists believe significantly understate the true level of household wealth.

However we choose to define Consuming China – or what one might cautiously call China's 'middle class' – one conclusion is clear: Chinese household consumption has crossed a critical threshold. China now has a globally significant number of consumers with genuine spending power. China's consumers still have a long way to go before they elbow out their American cousins as the engine of the global economy. The vast majority of the country still belong to Surviving China, and these people remain meaningless for foreign brands and retail chains. But rising household spending will contribute far more to China's growth over the coming decade than it did in the last.

China's consuming class of more than 300 million people is almost entirely made up of urban natives – those people who were born in the city and have an urban *hukou*. But as China's economy continues to grow and migrant incomes rise – and especially if China begins to make its much-needed *hukou* reforms – the new generation of urbanites should begin to follow their lead. BCG reckons that by 2020 nearly 800 Chinese cities will have real disposable per-capita incomes greater than Shanghai's in 2010. Genuine consumer culture has already moved from the wealthy cities of the eastern seaboard into provincial capitals like Chongqing, Chengdu and Wuhan. And over the coming decade, consumer culture is set to trickle down to the levels below.

The next wave of consumers will come from rapidly growing cities like Linyi in Shandong province. In marketing jargon, Linyi is a third- or fourth-tier city: a step below provincial capitals like Zhengzhou or Kunming, but large and wealthy enough to develop a meaningful core of consumers. Linyi's high street is typical of provincial cities throughout China, which are dominated by domestic clothes chains and by sportswear brands. Adidas and Nike, Li Ning and Anta, have opened thousands of franchise stores in tier-two cities and below since 2000, expanding quickly into places where most retailers feared to tread. For sportswear brands, market saturation means that the land rush has slowed. But for other types of retailer – notably big hypermarkets and fashion chains – interior China is precisely where new growth is coming from.

Modern retail chains and brands are busy expanding into cities that until recently were dominated by small, individually owned shops and traditional general stores. Between 2005 and 2010, the proportion of retail sales from modern-format stores – department stores, speciality stores, convenience stores, supermarkets and hypermarkets – jumped from roughly 15 per cent to 60 per cent. By 2010, China had 170,000 chain retailers nationwide, including 4,000 franchise businesses with hundreds of thousands of outlets. So far, this revolution has been concentrated in larger, more developed cities. In Chongqing city, consumers have several glitzy shopping malls to choose from, although there is far less choice than in the big cities of the east coast. But in neighbouring Fuling, a little over an hour's drive away, the retail market remains at least a decade behind. Aside from a couple of small department stores and an outlet of Suning, China's largest household appliance retailer, the city's streets are dominated by small family businesses, often selling single goods. The steep roads above the river are lined with shops selling bits and pieces for working men: steel tubes, hard hats, wires, rope, tools and tyres. Other shops flog wicker panniers, Chinese medicines or second-hand televisions. Meat, fruit and vegetables are sold in roadside markets, and there are plenty of places to buy cigarettes and drinks, or to slurp a quick bowl of noodles. Commercial life spills out onto the streets – but there are few national brands on show, let alone modern stores selling international goods.

China's retail sector remains highly fragmented: the vast majority of goods are sold in small, family-owned shops like those in Fuling. Modern retailing has made its biggest inroads in the grocery sector, which accounts for roughly two-thirds of all organized retail sales. Leading the charge are foreign hypermarkets, such as Carrefour, Walmart and Tesco. Although the top ten foreign retailers barely have 1,000 stores between them, they already rank among China's biggest retailers of non-durable items like groceries, packaged foods, soft drinks and toiletries. Much of that initial success came in the big, tier-one cities; but foreign hypermarkets are now well established in tier-two cities and are shifting their focus to tiers three and four. The momentum gathered pace in late 2008 when Beijing decentralized approval for store openings to local governments. Since then, foreign hypermarkets have opened several hundred stores in cities across the country.

Still, foreign hypermarkets have a long way to go before they win over the majority of China's shoppers. Sharp-eyed visitors to Beijing's branch of Sam's Club, a warehouse shopping club operated by US retail giant Walmart, can witness the challenge for modern retailing every weekend. Thousands of shoppers throng the store pushing bulging trolleys, much as they do in suburban shopping malls in America. But when they leave, many cross the road to the local wet market to stock up on fresh fruit and vegetables. Sam's Club maintains a decent selection of fresh produce, but local shoppers prefer the range and quality on offer in the traditional market.

The bustling wet market in Dongzhimen, a residential area in central Beijing, shows the value Chinese families place on freshness. Peering carefully into a fish tank, an old lady asks a rubber-booted fishmonger to scoop out a fat carp, which he swiftly knocks on the head, scours, guts, rinses and places in a black plastic bag. At the poultry stall, a middle-aged man requests a whole chicken chopped into little pieces, head and feet included. The stallholder plucks a fresh egg from the chicken's uterus, along with two yolky ovaries, and perfunctorily chops the bird up with a meat cleaver. The market is dominated by rows of large wooden trestle tables piled high with locally gown vegetables. 'I come here every day because it's much closer than the supermarket and the produce is cheaper and fresher,' comments one smartly dressed old lady, prodding a muddy radish.

Foreign supermarkets have adapted to local preferences by bringing some elements of the traditional wet market into their modern stores. Large hypermarket chains allow customers to squeeze and knead chunks of meat, and even let traditionally minded shoppers fish their own supper from live seafood tanks. Carrefour, like Walmart, offers a choice of pre- and non-packaged fresh food, allowing customers to size up the quality of individual vegetables and pieces of fruit, much as they would in a vegetable market. Many local supermarket chains also offer a reasonable selection of fresh meat, fish, fruit and vegetables. Yet most fresh food is still bought at traditional markets, which many shoppers visit on a daily basis. Street stalls selling fruit and vegetables are common in all city neighbourhoods, especially areas populated by migrant workers.

Nevertheless, the speed of expansion by the big foreign and domestic supermarket chains is impressive. It will take many years for China to develop a genuinely modern retail sector; but as China's consumer boom moves inexorably into lower-tier cities across the country's vast hinterland, the retail landscape will begin to look more like those in rich countries.

One piece of evidence is that, after years of inaction, international high-street brands are finally entering the market. Their previous reluctance reflected the peculiar structure of China's consumer goods market: for most of the past decade, this was bifurcated between premium-branded products at the top and no-brand products at the bottom, leaving a hole in the middle. This was no problem for hypermarkets, whose size enabled them to sell a wide variety of goods and beat smaller supermarket chains on price. But when it came to status-defining products like clothes and handbags, newly rich Chinese wanted to buy expensive brands – hence the success of luxury goods, which have been widely available in most second-tier cities for years. The bad news for mid-market brands was that these consumers remained extremely value-focused: office ladies would finance their Louis Vuitton bag by cutting expenditure on everything else. Consumers' obsession with aspirational purchases left little room for the type of high-street brands that dominate developed consumer markets.

Over the past five years, however, China's stunted middle market has finally started to bloom. Sweden's H&M, Japan's Uniqlo and Spain's Zara, which target affluent and fashionable young customers, have expanded quickly into second-tier cities since 2010. H&M only opened its first China store in 2007, but had eighty-nine stores in thirty-six cities by the end of 2012. Plugging the hole in the mid-market will take time, but foreign high-street chains are beginning to build a significant presence in provincial capitals. This is a far surer sign of genuine consumerism filtering down to China's interior than a handful of luxury brands flogging overpriced handbags.

Over the next decade, these mid-range brands will begin to follow Adidas and Nike into smaller cities, where fashion is currently dominated by local labels such as JeansWest and inexpensive Hong Kong brands like Giordano – both of which have stores in Linyi. These cheaper brands point the way forward for foreign fashion chains, much as the domestic sportswear brands pointed the way for Adidas and Nike, which followed their nimbler domestic rivals into China's interior. The enormous success of home-grown sportswear brands shows there is real money to be made in China's lower-tier cities. Anta Sports, China's second-largest domestic sportswear brand, had more than 7,000 franchised retail outlets and revenues in excess of US$1 billion in 2010. China Dongxiang, which owns the local rights to the Italian Kappa brand, habitually records annual operating profits of 40 per cent.

The success of sportswear brands like Anta is based on selling goods at significantly lower prices than foreign rivals and squeezing the life out of their franchisees. But a handful of domestic brands have created a lucrative foothold across China with self-owned stores selling pricier garments. The best example is Zhejiang-based Youngor, China's biggest domestic clothing brand, which recorded sales of US$5 billion in 2010, racking up a net profit of nearly US$1 billion. Youngor started life in 1979 as the Ningbo Youth Garment

Factory, a small workshop that employed 'rusticated youth' returning to the city after the Cultural Revolution to stitch together vests and shorts. Today Youngor International Garment City churns out 20 million casualwear items, 10 million shirts and 2 million suits every year, in what the company claims is the world's largest 'comprehensive clothing production base'.

Youngor has 1,500 outlets across the country, mainly targeting middle-aged men in rapidly urbanizing second- and third-tier cities. Even Youngor's flagship store on Shanghai's famous Nanjing Road is designed to appeal to domestic tourists from the provinces rather than to snootier locals. 'Wealthy people in Shanghai don't come here; they buy foreign brands,' admitted a saleswoman. But Youngor's smart shirts and suits are anything but cheap: the popular CEO line of shirts sell at US$100 each, while suits are priced from US$300 to US$1,500. Youngor's range varies nationwide, but the prices remain the same. For a government official, businessman or bridegroom in the provinces, Youngor is a smart way to make a good impression. The brand's success is evidence that that there are considerable numbers of consumers beyond China's biggest cities who are happy to fork out for a decent suit. As China's cities grow and household incomes rise, brands like Youngor are well positioned to take advantage.

Successfully straddling different urban markets will require considerable flexibility. Hypermarkets are already discovering that shoppers in third-tier cities like Linyi, where Carrefour is due to open a store, have different preferences from their wealthier customers in Beijing or Shanghai. They will also need to be agile to keep up with rapidly changing consumer demand. As soon as Nike and Adidas became popular in lower-tier cities, trendy shoppers in Shanghai and Beijing decided that sportswear was yesterday's fashion. Many younger migrant workers favour domestic sportswear brands, and may soon move on to foreign brands. When that happens, Adidas and Nike may find themselves relegated to providing casualwear for the urban working classes, much as they do in Western Europe today.

BOX 6.1   Want not, waste not

For a man born into rural poverty, Yu Changjiang is doing remarkably well. After twenty years of working in Chongqing, Yu has a local city *hukou*, owns his own 80-square-metre apartment, and brings home US$630 per month as a taxi driver. Adding in his wife's monthly wages of US$320, which she earns as a worker in one of Chongqing's many motorbike factories, the household pulls in over US$11,000 per year – twice that of the average migrant household.

Yu's residence status as a local *hukou* holder means he enjoys urban social security, including subsidized health care, and his daughter attends the neighbourhood school for free. Total annual living expenses for the Yu family, including mortgage repayments, amount to US$7,000. That leaves US$3,000 for potential consumption. But like so many Chinese families, they save almost every penny.

Yu's apartment on the southern edge of the city is light and airy, with a view over misty residential towers, derelict factories and vegetable patches. It consists of a large main room, two small bedrooms, and a tiny kitchen and bathroom. The furniture is the same as you would find in a rural home: hardwood sofas, a fold-up table, plastic stools. The household appliances – an old Changhong television, electric fans, a large Haier fridge and a washing machine – are also typical of the countryside. Yu did have a DVD player, but it broke. 'Now we just watch television,' he says.

The flat is austere, with bare walls and a hard-tiled floor, and there is almost no attempt to personalize the space. The only decoration is a clock, a wall calendar, a vase of fake flowers, and a porcelain figure of a Buddhist goddess. The bathroom has a squat lavatory and a shower that sprays directly onto the floor. The kitchen has a single hob. The only room that might look out of place in a typical village homestead is Yu's daughter's bedroom, which contains a desk and bookshelf, and a pair of yellow roller skates.

'I'd like a bigger television, I suppose, as this one's a bit small and old. And I'd like a bigger table to eat off,' Yu says. 'But I only buy things when I need them – otherwise it's just a waste of money.' He admits he spends little more on consumer goods as a city resident than his family back home in the village.

The only major difference in his daily lifestyle, Yu says, is diet. 'We eat meat every day. Farmers would never do that.' Yu's wife goes to the neighbourhood wet market every morning to pick up food for lunch, which might consist of duck's neck, rabbit or pigs' kidneys, plus vegetables, rice and plenty of fresh fruit. In the evenings, Yu eats out with other taxi drivers. They eat well, spending up to US$5 each.

'I haven't really changed much of my old way of thinking since I moved to the city,' Yu says. 'I'm somewhere in between a farmer and a city person. When I look at city people, I don't really feel I'm any different. But I do know there is an economic gap between us.'

These are positive developments: China's urban masses have more money in their pockets and are dressing better. Even ten years ago many Chinese cities remained drab places. Taking Beijing's subway was literally a colourless experience – a monochrome sea of black jackets and grey coats. The subway today lacks the visual variety of London or New York, but there is far more self-expression on show than ever before. Younger passengers dress in bright colours and sit glued to their iPhones, checking the latest gossip on Weibo, the Chinese version of Twitter. On a Saturday or Sunday night, the subway is packed with affluent 20-somethings returning home from a day of shopping or an evening at the cinema. What is true of Beijing today should be true of dozens of other cities tomorrow.

The main driving force behind this consumerist wave is rising incomes. Greater wealth is helping to foster a modern urban culture based around consumerism and individual identity – especially among young consumers in their twenties and thirties. Unlike their parents, who grew up in a revolutionary society with strong anti-consumerist values, the population born post-1970 came of age in an increasingly consumerist society. They are far more individualistic than their parents, and far readier to spend cash on personal hobbies and leisure pursuits. This sort of casual consumption simply did

BOX 6.2 Village life

Few of the thousands of people who drive down Beijing's east fourth ring road realize they are passing one of the capital's largest slums. Yet just a couple of kilometres south of the foreign enclave of Lido lies Xinzhuang, just one of an estimated 600 run-down urban 'villages' that house some of the city's 7 million migrant workers.

When Xinzhuang's residents return from a day selling fruit or servicing Beijing's expensive apartments, they socialize in the village. Everyone here is a migrant, so it is socially comfortable. And everything sold in the bustling street markets and makeshift shops – fresh fruit and vegetables, packaged food, shampoo, toilet rolls, clothes, shoes, pirated DVDs – is affordable. Filthy restaurants fry up delicious meals for as little as US$1; local-brand mobile phones sell for US$60. Many families in the village own an inexpensive computer or a cheap vehicle: the wasteland at the village edge is covered with delivery vans and local-brand cars. Like slums across the world, Xinzhuang village is a self-contained unit, a mini-economy operating independently of the rest of the city.

Aside from gossiping, there are three forms of entertainment in the village: drinking, surfing the Web, or hanging out at Black Eight pool bar. 'Some groups of young migrants come and play for fifteen hours at a stretch,' says Chen Jiaming, a Beijing local who runs the joint. 'This is the cheapest pool bar in Beijing, so they can afford it!' An hour on one of the three half-sized snooker tables costs US$1.50, and the bar is packed day and night.

Monthly incomes vary, but most migrants take home around US$400, higher than in many other cities. For younger migrants without children to provide for, that leaves a little cash for having fun. Dressed in jeans, trainers and T-shirts, many look similar to city residents. Any local can pick out an older migrant worker at a glance, but younger migrants can acclimatize quickly and are tougher to spot. For the present, these city newbies keep themselves to themselves, and only spend their limited cash in the village. But it would only take a few enlightened social policies and some extra dollars in their pocket to transform these young men and women into genuine consumers.

not exist until the last decade or so. But China is now in a position to follow the lead of Japan, Taiwan and South Korea, where daily consumption is a way of life.

If China manages the urbanization process effectively, the millions of migrants who flock to its cities each year will join this brave new consumerist world. From an economic as well as a social perspective, the rationale for treating rural migrants as second-class citizens is beginning to crumble. China's social model represses household consumption even as its leaders declare that consumption should drive future economic growth. They must find a way of fostering a healthier, more inclusive form of urbanization. If they do not, China's economic juggernaut could sputter to a halt.

CONCLUSION

Civilizing the Cities

The journey from farm to city is as old as civilization. In English, the term 'civilization' is derived from the Latin word for 'civil', which is itself related to the words for 'citizen' and 'city'. Etymologically at least, the process of moving to the city is by definition a civilizing experience – even if the road is long and hard. The best-known tale of migration in the English-speaking world is the fable of Dick Whittington, a poor country boy who travels to London to seek his fortune. When he arrives, he finds to his dismay that the streets are not paved with gold, as he had believed. Cold and hungry, he takes a job as a scullery boy, living in a rat-infested basement. But Dick finds a way of leveraging his only asset – his cat – and becomes a rich man (and, famously, thrice Lord Mayor of London). In the end, Dick finds that the city is indeed civilized: the streets really do glister with gold.

Millions of migrant workers and farmers in China today find themselves in a similar position to Dick Whittington at the start of his journey. Moving from farm to city promises potential riches far beyond what they can earn from tilling a small patch of earth, yet leaving behind the security of their land also means risking a life of urban hardship. More than 200 million migrant workers in China's cities live in shoddy housing and do tough, physical jobs. Like the boy in the story, they too have a potentially valuable asset: their land. But China's restrictive collective ownership laws mean that farmers can only squeeze out a fraction of their land's true worth. This condemns most rural migrants to beginning their urban life in poverty – a miserable state of affairs only exacerbated by China's discriminatory *hukou* system, which ensures that migrant workers live as second-class citizens.

Life for migrant workers in China's cities today is uncomfortable, unfair and insecure. But the economic rewards of moving to the city remain far greater than staying at home on the farm. *If* China's economy keeps growing and continues to provide enough jobs – admittedly a big *if* – mass migration to the cities will almost certainly continue, even without *hukou* reforms. By 2030, 1 billion Chinese citizens will live in cities. It is impossible to be sure what their life will be like; yet it is most unlikely that many will find the streets paved with gold.

How China's cities look in 2030 will depend on whether Chinese leaders are willing to forgo short-term economic gains and make the changes needed to create a healthier form of urbanization. One in three people living in China's cities today are not treated as equal citizens. If China does not begin to untie migrant workers' social-security entitlements from their *hukou* status, the proportion of disenfranchised urban residents will continue to grow. By 2030, almost half of China's billion urban citizens could effectively belong to a giant underclass, without proper housing or access to basic public services. The potentially explosive political ramifications of this bleak societal picture mean that some reform is unavoidable, as local governments have already found. The big question is whether the central government has the political will to address the roots of the problem. This will be a central question for the new administration under President Xi Jinping and Premier Li Keqiang to address.

So far, most of the running for reform has been made at the local level. Pilot land and *hukou* reforms in a number of cities and provinces have made some progress, although they have also confirmed fears about the inherent dangers of those reforms. Nevertheless, attempts in Chongqing and Chengdu to break down the urban–rural apartheid by relaxing *hukou* restrictions and firming up rural property rights are broadly positive moves, despite evidence of forced *hukou* conversions and illegal land grabs. These experiments are a necessary stage on the path to reform, even if they do have some unpleasant consequences. Seeing what works and what does not work is precisely their point.

Chengdu and Chongqing have already made some useful advances. Allowing farmers to sell their residential land rights to urban buyers is a small but important step towards unifying the rural and urban land markets. And enabling farmers to mortgage their land by providing land-use rights as collateral will help farmers unlock some of the dormant value in their land. Yet individual farmers still cannot sell the land they till, because it is not theirs to sell. It is indefensible that urban citizens should enjoy full individual property rights while farmers remain chained to village collectives. Collective ownership has patently failed to protect farmers from scheming local officials and village cadres. Any discussion of private ownership remains political dynamite, but the only logical trajectory of reform is to give individual farmers more rights over their land.

After two years of silence, the central government is once again talking about *hukou* reform. The State Council statement on *hukou* policy published in February 2012 was a broadly conservative document, warning cities not to move too quickly. But the instruction that local governments should no longer tie residents' eligibility for jobs, work training and schooling to their *hukou* status hinted at the direction of future reform. By 2030, policymakers should aim to grant all urban residents full social security and turn *hukou* into a simple family registration system, as it is in Taiwan and Japan. The proposal by the Ministry of Public Security to extend local residence permit schemes, which offer limited social benefits to migrant workers, is another small step in the right direction. Local *hukou* reforms have been slow and piecemeal, but more migrant children are receiving a state education, and more of their parents are enrolled in social insurance programmes.

The most encouraging new social policy in recent years is the national plan to build millions of units of subsidized public, or 'social', housing. This could, potentially, change the lives of China's urban poor. But the initial evidence suggests that most new units will go to local residents; few will be available to migrant workers without local *hukou*. As municipal governments demolish the thousands of slum villages that riddle China's cities, they must replace them with rental housing that migrant workers can afford. So far, China's urbanization process has not generated the kind of massive, cankerous slums that blight other developing cities around the world. But as more rural migrants bring their families to the city, and as these people begin to settle permanently, China's cities will struggle to avoid this horror. Despite investors' fears about China's supposed housing surplus, the more acute problem is China's housing shortage. More than 200 million migrant workers are currently excluded from China's housing market. As Chinese cities become more prosperous, these people should move out of slums and into social housing.

Yet subsidized housing is not a silver bullet. Cities with aggressive urbanization policies, such as Chongqing, need to beware herding millions of farmers into cities who have few, if any, useful urban skills. Long-term migrants know how to survive in the city; but many farmers will struggle. The fear is that they will end up living, unemployed and on benefits, in vast housing estates. This gloomy path is well trodden in the Western world: the USA has its drug-infested 'projects', the UK its sink council estates, and France its rundown *banlieues*. But China's policymakers have given little thought to the social canker that can fester among disadvantaged communities in public housing, especially where there is social discrimination and a shortage of jobs. In China the emphasis is on replacing decrepit housing with modern apartment blocks. But without very good management, towers of shoddily built flats peopled by hopeless ex-farmers could deteriorate quickly.

A more immediate concern is how cash-strapped cities will pay for all this new housing, not to mention the cost of integrating millions of migrants into city life. If ambitious local *hukou* reforms such as those in Chongqing are extended nationwide, the financial pressure will be intense. At the moment, local governments rely on land sales to plug their funding shortages. But this cannot be a long-term solution to the problem: China only has limited farmland and there is no guarantee that land prices will rise quickly enough to replenish local coffers. China must also consider the environmental impact of creating sprawling cities, especially as they will inevitably become clogged with millions of private cars. China is not America: it simply does not have enough land for every household to own its own vehicle. As the urban population grows ever larger, China must learn to accommodate people in highly concentrated cities that use limited resources efficiently.

If local governments cannot rely on flogging land to shore up rickety local finances, how will they pay for social housing, public services and city infrastructure? The answer is that the central government must shoulder its fair share of the spending burden. Local governments currently finance nearly all public services, including 80 per cent of basic health and education expenditure. Since a large slice of locally collected taxes goes into central government coffers, most local authorities struggle to meet their financial responsibilities. By contrast, the central government is swimming in cash. Increasingly, the challenge facing China is not a lack of funds as such, but how to channel them to the right places and to the right people. That means reforming the country's dysfunctional fiscal system so that the central government covers more social welfare, education and health services spending.

These are all big, difficult and painful reforms. Abandoning collectivist land ownership, dismantling the current *hukou* system and redesigning the country's fiscal system will require enormous political courage. So far, China's leaders have not shown the stomach to press ahead with such reforms. We can only hope that the new administration, which is set to hold power over the coming decade, will have more courage. The alternative is for China to become a kind of giant Latin America: a country with pockets of extreme wealth and an educated middle class, but whose cities teem with enormous slums and suppurate with entrenched social divisions.

Since 1978, China's leaders have made all the necessary changes to ensure that the country's economic growth machine kept purring along. It is now time to make some more. The fact that China's cities grew by 500 million people during that time without sparking greater social unrest is a remarkable achievement. But the present model cannot continue. If China's cities are truly to accommodate 1 billion residents – one in every eight people on the planet – its leaders must find a healthier, more inclusive and, ultimately, sustainable model of urban development. Only then will China's cities be truly civilized.

Bibliography

SOURCES IN ENGLISH

Anderlini, Jamil, 'Call to end China citizen registration system', *Financial Times* (1 March 2010).

Anderlini, Jamil, 'China's city population outstrips countryside', *Financial Times* (17 January 2012).

Batson, Andrew, 'Revisiting China's "empty city" of Ordos', *Wall Street Journal* (12 May 2010).

Bloomberg, 'China is on "treadmill to hell" as property prices will burst, Chanos says' (8 April 2010).

Bloomberg, 'Bo ouster undermines model to bridge China's wealth gap' (20 April 2012).

Bo Zhiyue et al., 'Bo Xilai and the Chongqing model', *EAI Background Brief* No. 465 (17 July 2009).

Boston Consulting Group, *The Keys to the Kingdom: Unlocking China's Consumer Power* (March 2010).

Branigan, Tania, 'Chinese newspapers in joint call to end curb on migrant workers', *Guardian* (1 March 2010).

Branigan, Tania, 'China becomes an urban nation at breakneck speed', *Guardian* (2 October 2011).

Buckley, Chris, 'Chinese village activist's death suspicious – daughter', Reuters (16 December 2011).

Buckley, Chris, et al., 'China bets future on inland cities', Reuters (3 August 2010).

Cai Fang, 'China's next giant: Urbanized migrants as new consumers', *China Economist* (September–October 2010): 82-7.

Cervero, Robert, 'Efficient urbanization: Economic performance and the shape of the metropolis', Lincoln Institute of Land Policy, Cambridge MA (2000).

Chan, Aris, 'Paying the price for economic development: The children of migrant workers in China', *China Labour Bulletin* (November 2009).

Chan, Kam Wing, 'City populations: Measuring the urban millions', *China Economic Quarterly* (March 2009): 21–6.

Chan, Kam Wing, 'Fundamentals of China's urbanization and policy', *China Review* 10(1) (Spring 2010): 63–93.

Chan, Kam Wing, 'The household registration system and migrant labor in China: Notes on a debate', *Population and Development Review* 36(2) (June 2010): 357–64.

Chan, Kam Wing, 'China, internal migration' (May 2011). Forthcoming in Immanuel Ness and Peter Bellwood (eds), *The Encyclopedia of Global Migration*, Blackwell, Oxford.

Chan, Kam Wing, 'Crossing the 50 percent population Rubicon: Can China urbanize to prosperity?', *Eurasian Geography and Economics* 53(1) (2012): 63–86.

Chan, Kam Wing, et al., 'Is China abolishing the *hukou* system?', *China Quarterly* (2008): 582–607.

Chang, Leslie, *Factory Girls: From Village to City in a Changing China*, Spiegel & Grau, New York (2008).

Chen Changsheng, et al., 'Migrant workers' citizenization creates demand for consumption', *China Economics* 28 (Sept–Oct 2010).

Chen Xiaoyan, 'Monitoring and evaluation in China's urban planning system: A case study of Xuzhou', prepared for *Planning Sustainable Cities: Global Report on Human Settlements 2009*, UN Habitat, London (2009).

Dalmia, Shikha, 'China's beauty problem: India's ugly cities are less cruel to their rural migrants than China's plush ones', Reason.com (23 February 2011).

de Soto, Hernando, *The Mystery of Capital: Why Capitalism Triumphs in the West and Fails Everywhere Else*, Basic Books, New York (2000).

Dyer, Geoff, 'China: No one home', *Financial Times* (21 February 2010).

The Economist, 'Migration in China: Invisible and heavy shackles' (6 May 2010).

The Economist, 'Urbanisation: Where do you live?' (23 June 2011).

Fewsmith, Joseph, 'Tackling the land issue – carefully', *China Leadership Monitor* 27 (2009): 1–8.

Ford, Peter, 'Beijing school closures leave thousands of migrant children without classrooms', *Christian Science Monitor* (26 August 2011).

Foster, Peter, et al., 'Underground world hints at China's coming crisis', *Telegraph* (30 January 2011).

Freeman, Will, 'Land reform: A controlled land "revolution"', *China Economic Quarterly* (December 2008): 7–8.

Freeman, Will, 'Land prices take off, but not as Beijing intended', *DragonWeek*,

GK Dragonomics (13 December 2010).

Gong Jing, et al., 'Sprawling Beijing tries a softer urbanization', *Caixin* (26 April 2010).

Green, Stephen, 'China – Chongqing's experimental land reforms, Part 1', Standard Chartered, *On the Ground* (25 February 2010).

Green, Stephen, 'China – Chongqing's experimental land reforms, Part 2', Standard Chartered, *On the Ground* (15 March 2010).

Green, Stephen, 'China – Chongqing's 2.4mn new renters', Standard Chartered, *On the Ground* (29 March 2011).

Green, Stephen, 'China – Rural land transfers.com', Standard Chartered, *On the Ground* (19 April 2011).

Gu Chaolin et al., 'China's master planning system in transition: Case study on Beijing', 46th ISOCARP Congress (2010).

Harney, Alexandra, *The China Price: The True Cost of Chinese Competitive Advantage*, Penguin, New York (2008).

Hessler, Peter, *River Town: Two Years on the Yangtze*, John Murray, London (2002).

Hessler, Peter, *Country Driving: A Journey Through China from Farm to Factory*, Harper, New York (2010).

Hille, Kathrin, 'Beijing pays for Chongqing confidence boost', *Financial Times* (9 May 2012).

Hokenson, RF, 'Migrant labour flows: Measuring the tide', *China Economic Quarterly* (September 2005): 23–8.

Hu Jing, 'A Critique of Chongqing's New "Land Reform"', *China Left Review* 1 (2008), trans. China Study Group.

Huang, Philip, 'Chongqing: Equitable development driven by a 'third hand', *Modern China* 37(6) (2011): 569–622.

Huang, Yasheng, *Capitalism with Chinese Characteristics: Entrepreneurship and the State*, Cambridge University Press, New York (2008).

JP Morgan, 'Urbanization, *hukou* reform and investment implications', *Hands-On China Report* (13 March 2012).

Jacob, Rahul, 'Wukan vows to foster tradition of free elections', *Financial Times* (3 February 2012).

Jacobs, Andrew, 'Chinese editorials assail a government system', *New York Times* (1 March 2010).

Jacobs, Andrew, 'China takes aim at rural influx', *New York Times* (29 August 2011a).

Jacobs, Andrew, 'Village revolts over inequities of Chinese life', *New York Times* (14 December 2011b)

Kirkby, R.J.R., *Urbanisation in China: Town and Country in a Developing Economy 1949–2000 AD*, Croom Helm, London (1985).

Kroeber, Arthur, 'Economic rebalancing: The end of surplus labor', *China Economic Quarterly* (March 2010): 35–46.

Kroeber, Arthur, 'Exploding the local-government debt myth', *China Insight: Economics*, GK Dragonomics (18 June 2010).

Kroeber, Arthur, 'Chinese consumers: Dream come true', *China Economic Quarterly* (December 2010): 17–23.

Kroeber, Arthur, 'The great rebalancing (II) – does China consume too little?', GK Dragonomics, *China Insight: Economics* (15 September 2011).

Kynge, James, *China Shakes the World: The Rise of a Hungry Nation*, W&N, London (2006).

Lan Fang et al., 'For migrants, Beijing school bells fall silent', *Caixin* (10 August 2011).

Landesa, 'China's farmers benefiting from land tenure reform', press release (24 February 2011).

Larmer, Brook, 'Building the American Dream in China', *New York Times* (16 March 2012).

Li Cheng, 'Hu Jintao's land reform: Ambition, ambiguity, and anxiety', *China Leadership Monitor* 27 (2009): 1–22.

McKeigue, James, 'China is heading for a brick wall, says Nouriel Roubini', *MoneyWeek* (13 May 2011).

McKinsey Global Institute, *Preparing for China's Urban Billion* (March 2009a).

McKinsey Global Institute, *If You've Got It, Spend It: Unleashing the Chinese Consumer* (August 2009b).

McKinsey Global Institute, *Urban World: Mapping the Economic Power of Cities* (March 2011).

Miller, Tom, '*Hukou* Reform: One step forward...', *China Economic Quarterly* (September 2005): 23–8.

Miller, Tom, 'Case studies I. Wuhan: Future megacity', *China Economic Quarterly* (March 2009): 32–5.

Miller, Tom, 'Development models: Big cities, small cities', *China Economic Quarterly* (March 2009): 27–31.

Miller, Tom, 'Pearl River Delta: Bloodied but unbowed', *China Economic Quarterly* (June 2009): 37–43

Miller, Tom, 'Ground-level truths on investment and consumption', *DragonWeek*, GK Dragonomics (11 January 2010).

Miller, Tom, 'Rural consumption: Little bang for the farming buck', *China Economic Quarterly* (June 2010): 41–5.

Miller, Tom, 'Sichuan: The never-ending investment story', *China Economic Quarterly* (September 2010): 51–7.

Miller, Tom, 'Retail market: Sportin' life', *China Economic Quarterly* (December 2010): 24–30.

Miller, Tom, 'Urbanization: Turning country bumpkins into city slickers', *China Economic Quarterly* (March 2011): 39–44.

Miller, Tom, 'Chongqing – China's new model worker?', *China Insight:*

Economics, GK Dragonomics (1 June 2011).

Miller, Tom, 'Migrant workers: Second-class citizens', *China Economic Quarterly* (June 2011): 35–40.

Miller, Tom, 'Don't fear the suburbs: Understanding China's "ghost towns"', *China Insight: Economics*, GK Dragonomics (1 September 2011).

Miller, Tom, 'Ghost towns: Not so scary', *China Economic Quarterly* (September 2011): 39–45.

Miller, Tom, 'Social integration: Whose city', *China Economic Quarterly* (December 2011): 26–34.

Miller, Tom, 'Urban consumption: The migrant solution?', *China Economic Quarterly* (December 2011): 35–41.

Miller, Tom, 'Urban living: Unlovely cities', *China Economic Quarterly* (December 2011): 15–25.

Miller, Tom, 'From Wukan to Chongqing: The problem of Chinese land reform', *Reportage*, GK Dragonomics (17 February 2012).

Miller, Tom, 'At last, momentum for *hukou* reform', *Reportage*, GK Dragonomics (27 March 2012).

Miller, Tom, et al., 'Chongqing and Wuhan: China's Chicagos?' *China Economic Quarterly* (December 2009): 51–7.

Moore, Malcolm, 'Rebel Chinese village of Wukan "has food for ten days"', *Telegraph* (14 December 2011).

Moore, Malcolm, et al., 'China to create largest mega city in the world with 42 million people', *Telegraph* (24 January 2011).

National Bureau of Statistics, 'Communiqué of the National Bureau of Statistics of People's Republic of China on Major Figures of the 2010 Population Census' (28 April 2011).

Natural Resources Defense Council, *Smart Cities: Solutions for China's Rapid Urbanization* (December 2007).

Orlik, Tom, et al., 'Behind a Chinese city's growth, heavy debt', *Wall Street Journal* (23 April 2012).

Pan Haixiao, 'Implementing sustainable urban travel policies in China,' International Transport Forum, Discussion Paper 2011-12, OECD (May 2011).

Prosterman, Roy, et al., 'Land: Righting the wrongs', *China Economic Quarterly* (March 2004): 20–25.

Studwell, Joe, *The China Dream*, Profile Books, London (2002).

Tao Ran, 'China's land grab is undermining grassroots democracy', *Guardian* (16 December 2011a).

Wang Wei, 'Ant tribe swarms to new villages', *China Daily* (12 August 2010).

Watson, Andrew, 'Social security for China's migrant workers – providing for old age', *Journal of Current Chinese Affairs* (April 2009): 85–115.

Watts, Jonathan, *When a Billion Chinese Jump: Voices from the Frontline of Climate Change*, Faber & Faber, London (2011).

Wong, Christine, 'Fiscal reform: Paying for the harmonious society', *China*

Economic Quarterly (June 2010): 20–25.

World Bank, 'Urbanization policy in Chongqing Municipality: A framework note' (2009).

World Bank and Development Research Center, *China 2030: Building a Modern, Harmonious, and Creative High-Income Society* (2012).

Wu Fulong, 'Re-orientation of the city plan: Strategic planning and design competition in China', *Geoforum* 38 (2007): 379–92.

Wu Fulong, 'Gated and packaged suburbia: Packaging and branding Chinese suburban residential development', *Cities* 27 (2010): 385–96.

Xue, Jin, et al., 'The challenge of sustainable mobility in urban planning and development: A comparative study of the Copenhagen and Hangzhou metropolitan areas', *International Journal of Urban Sustainable Development* (2011): 1–22.

Yao, Rosealea, 'Managing local-government debt the Chongqing way', *Dragon-Week*, GK Dragonomics (4 May 2010).

Yao, Rosealea, 'How rigged land prices make factories cheap and homes dear', *DragonWeek*, GK Dragonomics (24 May 2010).

Yao, Rosealea, 'No room for squares: China's housing supply and demand', *China Insight: Economics*, GK Dragonomics (26 May 2011).

Yao, Rosealea, 'Property: A plague o' both your houses!', *China Economic Quarterly* (June 2011): 10–12.

SOURCES IN CHINESE

All-China Federation of Trade Unions, '2010 nian qiye xinshengdai nongmingong zhuangkuang diaocha yi duice jianyi' (February 2011).

Beijing Wanbao, '50 zhongdian cun mianei banqianwan chanye yongdishang kejian gongzufang' (1 April 2010).

Caijing, 'Hugai Chengdu tupo' (20 December 2010).

Caijing, 'Xintugai Chengdu lujing' (1 March 2011).

Caixin, 'Xu Chenggang: Tudi wenti wuke huibi' (13 April 2011)

Cui Zhiyuan, 'Chongqing "shida minsheng gongcheng" de zhengzhi jiingji xue', *Journal of the Party School of the Central Committee of the CPC* 14(5) (1 October 2010): 5-10.

Cui Zhiyuan, 'Cong weijiufang gaizao kan "Chongqing moshi"' (n.d.).

Cui Zhiyuan, 'Meiguo alasijiazhou changhahaode de Chongqing yuan' (n.d.).

Dahe Wang, 'Zhengdong xinqu – chuli yu zhengzhou de "dong fang mingzhu"' (1 June 2011).

Dazhong Daily, 'Jujiao Zhongguo chengzhenhua jianshe de "Linyi moshi"' (22 June 2011).

Development Research Center, *Nongmingong shiminhua: Zhidu chuangxin yu dingceng zhengce sheji*, Zhongguo Fazhan Chubanshe, Beijing (2011).

Development Research Center, 'Chongqingshi huji zhidu gaige qingkuang jieshao' (unpublished).

Jingji Daobao, '"Si da zhanlue" tuiding Linyi jingji kuayue fazhan' (4 July 2011).

Ministry of Land and Resources, '2011 nian shangbannian chachu guotu ziyuan lingyu weifa weigui anjian qingkuang' (12 July 2011).

Nanfang Bao, 'Yige Zhengzhou sizuo daxuecheng Zhengdong xinqu "gaoxiaoqu" guimo chuxian' (8 August 2006).

Nanfang Zhoumo, 'Huobao dipiao turan zanting, Chengdu tugai fengxiang nanbian' (30 December 2010).

National Bureau of Statistics, *'Xin shengdai nongmingong de shuzi, jiegou he tedian'* (11 March 2011).

National Bureau of Statistics, '2011 nian wo guo nongmingong diaocha lince baogao' (27 April 2012).

National Population and Family Planning Commission of China, *Liudong renkou fazhan baogao 2011*, Zhongguo Renkou Chubanshe, Beijing (2011).

Ordos City Government, 'E'erduosishi zhengfu gongzuo baogao 2011' (2012).

Qilu Wanbao, 'Tanfang chengxiang yitihua de "Linyi moshi"' (30 March 2010).

Renmin Wang, 'Linyishi chengxiang jianshe yongdi zengjain guagou zai xianxin pianzhang' (26 January 2011).

Renmin Wang, 'Jujiao Zhengzhou dushi qu jianshe zoujin Zhengdong xinqu' (25 May 2011).

State Council, 'Guowuyuan guanyu yange guifan chengxiang jianshe yongdi zengjian guagou shidian qieshi zuohao nongcun tudi zhengzhi gongzuo de tongzhi' (2010).

State Council, 'Guowuyuan bangongting guanyu jiji wentuo tuijin huji guanli zhidu gaige de tongzhi (2011)' (23 February 2012).

State Council, 'Huji guanli zhidu gaige de tongzhi, guo banfa (2011)' (26 February 2011).

Su Wei et al., *Chongqing moshi*, China Economic Publishing House, Beijing (2011).

Tao Ran, 'Chengshihua moshi yu tudi zhidu gaige: Dianxing shishi, zhuyao tiaozhan yu zhengce tupo', Brookings-Tsinghua Center for Public Policy (September 2011b).

Xin Shiji, 'Chengdu gongbu huji gaige shijian biao' (17 November 2010).

Xin Shiji, 'Tudi huan huji jiaoting' (31 January 2011).

Xin Shiji, 'Huji gaige jiangwen' (21 March 2011).

Xin Shiji, 'Chen Xiwen: Tuijin chengzhenhua buneng sunhai nongmin quanyi' (6 November 2011).

Zhongguo Jingji Shibao, 'Chongqing "dipiao" diaocha' (20 May 2011).

Index